T0314921

Yield Curve Modeling and Forecasting

THE ECONOMETRIC AND TINBERGEN INSTITUTES LECTURES

Series Editors
Herman K. van Dijk and Philip Hans Franses
The Econometric Institute,
Erasmus University Rotterdam

The *Econometric Institute Lectures* series is a joint project of Princeton University Press and the Econometric Institute at Erasmus University Rotterdam.

This series collects the lectures of leading researchers which they have given at the Econometric Institute for an audience of academics and students.

The lectures are at a high academic level and deal with topics that have important policy implications. The series covers a wide range of topics in econometrics. It is not confined to any one area or sub-discipline.

The Econometric Institute is the leading research center in econometrics and management science in the Netherlands. The Institute was founded in 1956 by Jan Tinbergen and Henri Theil, with Theil being its first director. The Institute has received worldwide recognition with an advanced training program for various degrees in econometrics.

Other books in this series include

Anticipating Correlations: A New Paradigm for Risk Management by Robert Engle

Complete and Incomplete Econometric Models by John Geweke

Social Choice with Partial Knowledge of Treatment Response by Charles F. Manski

Yield Curve Modeling and Forecasting

The Dynamic Nelson-Siegel Approach

Francis X. Diebold and Glenn D. Rudebusch

Princeton University Press
Princeton and Oxford

Published by Princeton University Press,
41 William Street, Princeton, New Jersey 08540
In the United Kingdom: Princeton University Press,
6 Oxford Street, Woodstock, Oxfordshire OX20 1TW

press.princeton.edu

Library of Congress Cataloging-in-Publication Data

Diebold, Francis X., 1959–
   Yield curve modeling and forecasting:
   the dynamic Nelson-Siegel approach /
   Francis X. Diebold, Glenn D. Rudebusch.
      p. cm. - (The Econometric and Tinbergen Institutes lectures)
   Includes bibliographical references and index.
   ISBN 978-0-691-14680-5 (hardcover: alk. paper)
   1. Bonds—Mathematical models.
   I. Rudebusch, Glenn D., 1959– II. Title.

HG4651.D537 2013
332.63′2042—dc23   2012020360

British Library Cataloging-in-Publication Data is available

This book has been composed in Computer Modern using TeX
Typeset by T&T Productions Ltd, London

10 9 8 7 6 5 4 3 2 1

To our wives

Contents

Illustrations

Figures

Tables

Introduction

The Econometric and Tinbergen Institute Lectures deal with topics in econometrics that have important policy implications. The lectures cover a wide range of topics and are not confined to any one area or subdiscipline. Leading international scientists in the fields of econometrics in which applications play a major role are invited to give three-day lectures on a topic to which they have contributed significantly.

The 2012 lectures deal with the topic of describing and modeling the dynamic behavior of a large cross section of financial assets, such as Treasury bonds. Understanding their evolution is crucial for implied policy analysis. The understanding refers to expectation and pricing mechanisms that are part of the so-called Nelson-Siegel approach and the implied policy analysis deals with such topics as dynamic portfolio allocation and hedging investment risks of financial assets. Frank Diebold and Glenn Rudebusch have written a lucid book on these topics that are situated at the interface of macroeconomics and finance. Results of their research, reported in this book, are relevant for academic researchers as well as professionals in the banking and financial sector.

As editors of the series we are indebted to the Econometric and Tinbergen Institutes for continued support for the series.

Philip Hans Franses and Herman K. van Dijk
Econometric and Tinbergen Institutes
Erasmus School of Economics

Preface

Understanding the dynamic evolution of the yield curve is important for many tasks, including pricing financial assets and their derivatives, managing financial risk, allocating portfolios, structuring fiscal debt, conducting monetary policy, and valuing capital goods. To investigate yield curve dynamics, researchers have produced a huge literature with a wide variety of models. In our view it would be neither interesting nor desirable to produce an extensive survey. Indeed our desire is precisely the opposite: We have worked hard to preserve the sharp focus of our Econometric Institute and Tinbergen Institute (EITI) Lectures, delivered in Rotterdam in June 2010, on which this book is based.

Our sharp focus is driven by an important observation: Most yield curve models tend to be either theoretically rigorous but empirically disappointing, or empirically successful but theoretically lacking. In contrast, we emphasize in this book two intimately related extensions of the classic yield curve model of Nelson and Siegel (1987). The first is a dynamized version, which we call "dynamic Nelson-Siegel" (DNS). The second takes DNS and makes it arbitrage-free; we call it "arbitrage-free Nelson-Siegel" (AFNS). Indeed the two models are just slightly different implementations of a single, unified approach to dynamic yield curve modeling and forecasting. DNS has been highly successful empirically and can easily be made arbitrage-free (i.e., converted to AFNS) if and when that is desirable.

Our intended audience is all those concerned with bond markets and their links to the macroeconomy, whether researchers, practitioners, or students. It spans academic economics and finance, central banks and NGOs, government, and industry. Our methods are of special relevance for those interested in asset pricing, portfolio allocation, and risk management.

We use this book, just as we used the EITI Lectures, as an opportunity to step back from the signposts of individual journal articles and assess the broader landscape—where we've been, where we are, and where we're going in terms of the whats and whys and hows of yield curve modeling, all through a DNS lens. Our methods and framework have strong grounding in the best of the past, yet simultaneously they are very much intertwined with the current research frontier and actively helping to push it outward.

We begin with an overview of yield curve "facts" and quickly move to the key fact: Beneath the high-dimensional set of observed yields, and guiding their evolution, is a much lower-dimensional set of yield factors. We then motivate DNS as a powerful approximation to that dynamic factor structure. We treat DNS yield curve modeling in a variety of contexts, emphasizing both descriptive aspects (in-sample fit, out-of-sample forecasting, etc.) and efficient-markets aspects (imposition of absence of arbitrage, whether and where one would *want* to impose absence of arbitrage, etc.). We devote special attention to the links between the yield curve and macroeconomic fundamentals.

We are pleased to have participated in the DNS research program with talented co-authors who have taught us much en route: Boragan Aruoba, Jens Christensen, Lei Ji, Canlin Li, Jose Lopez, Monika Piazzesi,

Eric Swanson, Tao Wu, and Vivian Yue. Christensen's influence, in particular, runs throughout this book.

We are truly indebted to Herman van Dijk and Dick van Dijk for their intellectual leadership in organizing the EITI Lectures. We are similarly indebted to the team at Princeton University Press, especially Seth Ditchik, for meticulous and efficient administration and production.

We are grateful to many colleagues and institutions for helpful input at various stages. In particular, we thank—without implicating in any way—Caio Almeida, Boragan Aruoba, Jens Christensen, Dick van Dijk, Herman van Dijk, Greg Duffee, Darrell Duffie, Jesús Fernández-Villaverde, Mike Gibbons, Jim Hamilton, Jian Hua, Lawrence Klein, Siem Jan Koopman, Leo Krippner, Jose Lopez, Andre Lucas, Emanuel Mönch, James Morley, Charles Nelson, Ken Singleton, Dongho Song, Jim Steeley, Chuck Whiteman, and Tao Wu. Several anonymous reviewers of the manuscript also provided insightful and valuable comments. For research assistance we thank Fei Chen, Jian Hua, and Eric Johnson. For financial support we are grateful to the National Science Foundation, the Wharton Financial Institutions Center, and the Guggenheim Foundation.

We hope that the book conveys a feeling for the excitement of the rapidly evolving field of yield curve modeling. That rapid evolution is related to, but no excuse for, any errors of commission and omission that surely remain, for which we apologize in advance.

Francis X. Diebold, Philadelphia 2011
fdiebold@sas.upenn.edu
www.ssc.upenn.edu/~fdiebold

Glenn D. Rudebusch, San Francisco 2011
glenn.rudebusch@sf.frb.org
www.frbsf.org/economics/economists/grudebusch

Additional Acknowledgment

This book draws on certain of our earlier-published papers, including:

Christensen, J.H.E., Diebold, F.X., and Rudebusch, G.D. (2009), "An Arbitrage-Free Generalized Nelson-Siegel Term Structure Model," *The Econometrics Journal*, 12, 33–64.

Christensen, J.H.E., Diebold, F.X., and Rudebusch, G.D. (2011), "The Affine Arbitrage-Free Class of Nelson-Siegel Term Structure Models," *Journal of Econometrics*, 164, 4–20.

Christensen, J.H.E., Lopez, J.A., and Rudebusch, G.D. (2010), "Inflation Expectations and Risk Premiums in an Arbitrage-Free Model of Nominal and Real Bond Yields," *Journal of Money, Credit, and Banking*, 42, 143–178.

Diebold, F.X., Ji, L., and Li, C. (2006), "A Three-Factor Yield Curve Model: Non-Affine Structure, Systematic Risk Sources, and Generalized Duration," in L.R. Klein (ed.), *Long-Run Growth abd Short-Run Stabilization: Essays in Memory of Albert Ando*, 240–274. Cheltenham, U.K.: Edward Elgar.

Diebold, F.X., and Li, C. (2006), "Forecasting the Term Structure of Government Bond Yields," *Journal of Econometrics*, 130, 337–364.

Diebold, F.X., Li, C., and Yue, V. (2008), "Global Yield Curve Dynamics and Interactions: A Generalized Nelson-Siegel Approach," *Journal of Econometrics*, 146, 351–363.

Diebold, F.X., Piazzesi, M., and Rudebusch, G.D. (2005), "Modeling Bond Yields in Finance and Macroeconomics," *American Economic Review*, 95, 415–420.

Diebold, F.X., Rudebusch, G.D., and Aruoba, B. (2006), "The Macroeconomy and the Yield Curve: A Dynamic Latent Factor Approach," *Journal of Econometrics*, 131, 309–338.

Rudebusch, G.D. (2010), "Macro-Finance Models of Interest Rates and the Economy," *The Manchester School*, 78, 25–52.

Rudebusch, G.D., and Swanson, E. (2008), "Examining the Bond Premium Puzzle with a DSGE Model," *Journal of Monetary Economics*, 55, S111–S126.

Rudebusch, G.D., and Swanson, E. (2012), "The Bond Premium in a DSGE Model with Long-Run Real and Nominal Risks," *American Economic Journal: Macroeconomics*, 4, 105–143.

Rudebusch, G.D., Swanson, E., and Wu, T. (2006), "The Bond Yield 'Conundrum' from a Macro-Finance Perspective," *Monetary and Economic Studies*, 24, 83–128.

Rudebusch, G.D., and Wu, T. (2007), "Accounting for a Shift in Term Structure Behavior with No-Arbitrage and Macro-Finance Models," *Journal of Money, Credit, and Banking*, 39, 395–422.

Rudebusch, G.D., and Wu, T. (2008), "A Macro-Finance Model of the Term Structure, Monetary Policy, and the Economy," *Economic Journal*, 118, 906–926.

Yield Curve Modeling and Forecasting

1

Facts, Factors, and Questions

In this chapter we introduce some important conceptual, descriptive, and theoretical considerations regarding nominal government bond yield curves. Conceptually, just what is it that are we trying to measure? How can we best understand many bond yields at many maturities over many years? Descriptively, how do yield curves tend to behave? Can we obtain simple yet accurate dynamic characterizations and forecasts? Theoretically, what governs and restricts yield curve shape and evolution? Can we relate yield curves to macroeconomic fundamentals and central bank behavior?

These multifaceted questions are difficult yet very important. Accordingly, a huge and similarly multifaceted literature attempts to address them. Numerous currents and cross-currents, statistical and economic, flow through the literature. There is no simple linear thought progression, self-contained with each step following logically from that before. Instead the literature is more of a tangled web; hence our intention is not to produce a "balanced" survey of yield curve modeling, as it is not clear whether that would be helpful or even what it would mean. On the contrary, in this book we slice through the literature in a calculated way, assembling and elaborating on a very particular approach to yield curve modeling. Our approach is simple yet rigorous, simultaneously in close touch with modern statistical and financial economic thinking, and effective in a variety of situations. But we are getting ahead of ourselves. First we must lay the groundwork.

1.1 Three Interest Rate Curves

Here we fix ideas, establish notation, and elaborate on key concepts by recalling three key theoretical bond market constructs and the relationships among them: the discount curve, the forward rate curve, and the yield curve. Let $P(\tau)$ denote the price of a τ-period discount bond, that is, the present value of \$1 receivable τ periods ahead. If $y(\tau)$ is its continuously compounded yield to maturity, then by definition

$$P(\tau) = e^{-\tau y(\tau)}. \tag{1.1}$$

Hence the discount curve and yield curve are immediately and fundamentally related. Knowledge of the discount function lets one calculate the yield curve.

The discount curve and the forward rate curve are similarly fundamentally related. In particular, the forward rate curve is defined as

$$f(\tau) = \frac{-P'(\tau)}{P(\tau)}. \tag{1.2}$$

Thus, just as knowledge of the discount function lets one calculate the yield curve, so too does knowledge of the discount function let one calculate the forward rate curve.

Equations (1.1) and (1.2) then imply a relationship between the yield curve and forward rate curve,

$$y(\tau) = \frac{1}{\tau} \int_0^\tau f(u)du. \tag{1.3}$$

In particular, the zero-coupon yield is an equally weighted average of forward rates.

The upshot for our purposes is that, because knowledge of any one of $P(\tau)$, $y(\tau)$, and $f(\tau)$ implies knowledge of the other two, the three are effectively interchangeable. Hence with no loss of generality one can choose to work with $P(\tau)$, $y(\tau)$, or $f(\tau)$. In this book, following much of both academic and industry practice, we work with the yield curve, $y(\tau)$. But again, the choice is inconsequential in theory.

Complications arise in practice, however, because although we observe prices of traded bonds with various amounts of time to maturity, we do not directly observe yields, let alone the zero-coupon yields at fixed standardized maturities (e.g., six-month, ten-year, ...), with which we work throughout. Hence we now provide some background on yield construction.

1.2 Zero-Coupon Yields

In practice, yield curves are not observed. Instead, they must be estimated from observed bond prices. Two historically popular approaches to constructing yields proceed by fitting a smooth discount curve and then converting to yields at the relevant maturities using formulas (1.2) and (1.3).

The first discount curve approach to yield curve construction is due to McCulloch (1971, 1975), who models the discount curve using polynomial splines.[1] The fitted discount curve, however, diverges at long maturities due to the polynomial structure, and the corresponding yield curve inherits that unfortunate property. Hence

---

[1] See also McCulloch and Kwon (1993).

such curves can provide poor fits to yields that flatten out with maturity, as emphasized by Shea (1984).

An improved discount curve approach to yield curve construction is due to Vasicek and Fong (1982), who model the discount curve using exponential splines. Their clever use of a negative transformation of maturity, rather than maturity itself, ensures that forward rates and zero-coupon yields converge to a fixed limit as maturity increases. Hence the Vasicek-Fong approach may be more successful at fitting yield curves with flat long ends.

Notwithstanding the progress of Vasicek and Fong (1982), discount curve approaches remain potentially problematic, as the implied forward rates are not necessarily positive. An alternative and popular approach to yield construction is due to Fama and Bliss (1987), who construct yields not from an estimated discount curve, but rather from estimated forward rates at the observed maturities. Their method sequentially constructs the forward rates necessary to price successively longer-maturity bonds. Those forward rates are often called "unsmoothed Fama-Bliss" forward rates, and they are transformed to unsmoothed Fama-Bliss yields by appropriate averaging, using formula (1.3). The unsmoothed Fama-Bliss yields exactly price the included bonds. Unsmoothed Fama-Bliss yields are often the "raw" yields to which researchers fit empirical yield curves, such as members of the Nelson-Siegel family, about which we have much to say throughout this book. Such fitting effectively smooths the unsmoothed Fama-Bliss yields.

1.3   Yield Curve Facts

At any time, dozens of different yields may be observed, corresponding to different bond maturities. But yield curves evolve dynamically; hence they have not only a cross-sectional, but also a temporal, dimension.[2] In this section we address the obvious descriptive question: How do yields tend to behave across different maturities and over time?

The situation at hand is in a sense very simple—modeling and forecasting a time series—but in another sense rather more complex and interesting, as the series to be modeled is in fact a series of *curves*.[3] In Figure 1.1 we show the resulting three-dimensional surface for the United States, with yields shown as a function of maturity, over time. The figure reveals a key yield curve fact: yield curves move a lot, shifting among different shapes: increasing at increasing or decreasing rates, decreasing at increasing or decreasing rates, flat, U-shaped, and so on.

Table 1.1 presents descriptive statistics for yields at various maturities. Several well-known and important yield curve facts emerge. First, time-averaged yields (the "average yield curve") increase with maturity; that is, term premia appear to exist, perhaps due to risk aversion, liquidity preferences, or preferred habitats. Second, yield volatilities decrease with maturity, presumably because long rates involve averages of expected future short rates. Third, yields are highly persistent, as evidenced not only by the very large 1-month autocorrelations but also by the sizable 12-month autocorrelations.

---

[2] We will be interested in dynamic modeling and forecasting of yield curves, so the temporal dimension is as important as the variation across bond maturity.

[3] The statistical literature on functional regression deals with sets of curves and is therefore somewhat related to our concerns. See, for example, Ramsay and Silverman (2005) and Ramsay et al. (2009). But the functional regression literature typically does not address dynamics, let alone the many special nuances of yield curve modeling. Hence we are led to rather different approaches.

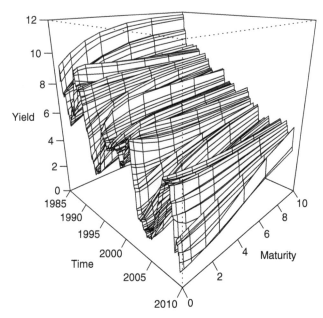

Figure 1.1. Bond Yields in Three Dimensions. We plot end-of-month U.S. Treasury bill and bond yields at maturities ranging from 6 months to 10 years. Data are from the Board of Governors of the Federal Reserve System, based on Gürkaynak et al. (2007). The sample period is January 1985 through December 2008.

Table 1.2 shows the same descriptive statistics for yield *spreads* relative to the 10-year bond. Yield spread dynamics contrast rather sharply with those of yield levels; in particular, spreads are noticeably less volatile and less persistent. As with yields, the 1-month spread autocorrelations are very large, but they decay more quickly, so that the 12-month spread autocorrelations are noticeably smaller than those for yields. Indeed many strategies for active bond trading (sometimes successful and sometimes not!) are based on spread reversion.

Table 1.1. Bond Yield Statistics

Maturity (months)	$\bar{y}$	$\hat{\sigma}_y$	$\hat{\rho}_y(1)$	$\hat{\rho}_y(12)$
6	4.9	2.1	0.98	0.64
12	5.1	2.1	0.98	0.65
24	5.3	2.1	0.97	0.65
36	5.6	2.0	0.97	0.65
60	5.9	1.9	0.97	0.66
120	6.5	1.8	0.97	0.68

Notes: We present descriptive statistics for end-of-month yields at various maturities. We show sample mean, sample standard deviation, and first- and twelfth-order sample autocorrelations. Data are from the Board of Governors of the Federal Reserve System. The sample period is January 1985 through December 2008.

1.4 Yield Curve Factors

Multivariate models are required for sets of bond yields. An obvious model is a vector autoregression or some close relative. But unrestricted vector autoregressions are profligate parameterizations, wasteful of degrees of freedom. Fortunately, it turns out that financial asset returns typically conform to a certain type of *restricted* vector autoregression, displaying *factor structure*. Factor structure is said to be operative in situations where one sees a high-dimensional object (e.g., a large set of bond yields), but where that high-dimensional object is driven by an underlying lower-dimensional set of objects, or "factors." Thus beneath a high-dimensional seemingly complicated set of observations lies a much simpler reality.

Indeed factor structure is ubiquitous in financial markets, financial economic theory, macroeconomic funda-

Table 1.2.   Yield Spread Statistics

Maturity (months)	$\bar{s}$	$\hat{\sigma}_s$	$\hat{\rho}_s(1)$	$\hat{\rho}_s(12)$
6	−1.6	1.3	0.98	0.44
12	−1.4	1.1	0.98	0.46
24	−1.1	0.9	0.97	0.48
36	−0.9	0.7	0.97	0.47
60	−0.6	0.4	0.96	0.44
120	NA	NA	NA	NA

Notes: We present descriptive statistics for end-of-month yield spreads (relative to the 10-year bond) at various maturities. We show sample mean, sample standard deviation, and first- and twelfth-order sample autocorrelations. Data are from the Board of Governors of the Federal Reserve System, based on Gürkaynak et al. (2007). The sample period is January 1985 through December 2008.

mentals, and macroeconomic theory. Campbell et al. (1997), for example, discuss aspects of empirical factor structure in financial markets and theoretical factor structure in financial economic models.[4] Similarly, Aruoba and Diebold (2010) discuss empirical factor structure in macroeconomic fundamentals, and Diebold and Rudebusch (1996) discuss theoretical factor structure in macroeconomic models.

In particular, factor structure provides a fine description of the term structure of bond yields.[5] Most early studies involving mostly long rates implicitly adopt a single-factor world view (e.g., Macaulay (1938)), where the factor is the level (e.g., a long rate). Similarly, early

---

[4] Interestingly, asset pricing in the factor framework is closely related to asset pricing in the pricing kernel framework, as discussed in Chapter 11 of Singleton (2006).

[5] For now we do not distinguish between government and corporate bond yields. We will consider credit risk spreads later.

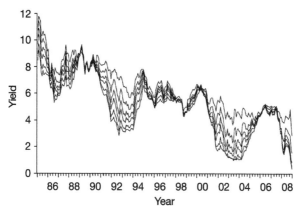

Figure 1.2. Bond Yields in Two Dimensions. We plot end-of-month U.S. Treasury bill and bond yields at maturities of 6, 12, 24, 36, 60, and 120 months. Data are from the Board of Governors of the Federal Reserve System, based on Gürkaynak et al. (2007). The sample period is January 1985 through December 2008.

arbitrage-free models like Vasicek (1977) involve only a single factor. But single-factor structure severely limits the scope for interesting term structure dynamics, which rings hollow in terms of both introspection and observation.

In Figure 1.2 we show a time-series plot of a standard set of bond yields. Clearly they *do* tend to move noticeably together, but at the same time, it's clear that more than just a common level factor is operative. In the real world, term structure data—and, correspondingly, modern empirical term structure models—involve *multiple* factors. This classic recognition traces to Litterman and Scheinkman (1991), Willner (1996), and Bliss (1997), and it is echoed repeatedly in the literature. Joslin et al. (2010), for example, note:

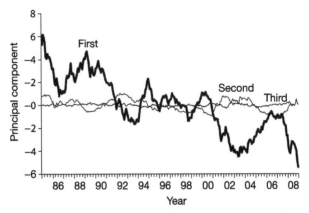

Figure 1.3. Bond Yield Principal Components. We show the first, second, and third principal components of bond yields in dark, medium, and light shading, respectively.

> The cross-correlations of bond yields are well described by a low-dimensional factor model in the sense that the first three principal components of bond yields . . . explain well over 95 percent of their variation. . . . Very similar three-factor representations emerge from arbitrage-free, dynamic term structure models . . . for a wide range of maturities.

Typically three factors, or principal components, are all that one needs to explain most yield variation. In our data set the first three principal components explain almost 100 percent of the variation in bond yields; we show them in Figure 1.3 and provide descriptive statistics in Table 1.3.

The first factor is borderline nonstationary. It drifts downward over much of the sample period, as inflation was reduced relative to its high level in the early 1980s. The first factor is the most variable but also the most predictable, due to its very high persistence. The second factor is also highly persistent and displays a clear

Table 1.3. Yield Principal Components Statistics

PC	$\hat{\sigma}$	$\hat{\rho}(1)$	$\hat{\rho}(12)$	R^2
First	2.35	0.97	0.67	0.98
Second	0.52	0.97	0.45	0.95
Third	0.10	0.83	0.15	0.70

Notes: We present descriptive statistics for the first three principal components of end-of-month U.S. government bill and bond yields at maturities of 6, 12, 24, 36, 60, and 120 months. We show principal component sample standard deviation, first- and twelfth-order principal component sample autocorrelations, and the predictive R^2 (see Diebold and Kilian (2001)) from an $AR(p)$ approximating model with p selected using the Schwartz criterion. Data are from the Board of Governors of the Federal Reserve System, based on Gürkaynak et al. (2007). The sample period is January 1985 through December 2008.

business cycle rhythm. The second factor is less variable, less persistent, and less predictable than the level factor. The third factor is the least variable, least persistent, and least predictable.

In Figure 1.4 we plot the three principal components (factors) against standard empirical yield curve level, slope, and curvature measures (the 10-year yield, the 10Y-6M spread, and a 6M+10Y-2*5Y butterfly spread, respectively). The figure reveals that the three bond yield factors effectively *are* level, slope, and curvature. This is important, because it implies that the different factors likely have different and specific macroeconomic determinants. Inflation, for example, is clearly related to the yield curve level, and the stage of the business cycle is relevant for the slope. It is also noteworthy that the yield factors are effectively orthogonal due to their exceptionally close links to the principal components, which are orthogonal by construction.

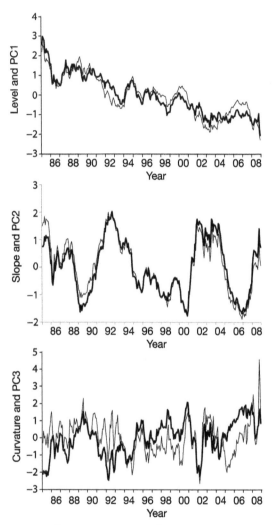

Figure 1.4. Empirical Level, Slope, and Curvature and First Three Principal Components of Bond Yields. We show the standardized empirical level, slope, and curvature with dark lines, and the first three standardized principal components (denoted PC1, PC2, and PC3) with lighter lines.

The disproportionate amount of yield variation associated with the common *level* factor, together with its high persistence, explains the broad sweep of earlier-discussed facts, in particular the high persistence of yields and the greatly reduced persistence of yield spreads (because the common level factor vanishes from the spreads). Reality is of course a bit more complicated, as slope and curvature factors are also operative, but the effects of the level factor dominate.

A factor structure for yields with a highly persistent level factor is constrained by economic theory. Economic theory strongly suggests that nominal bond yields should not have unit roots, because the yields are bounded below by zero, whereas unit-root processes have random walk components and therefore will eventually cross zero almost surely. Nevertheless, the unit root may be a good approximation so long as yields are not too close to zero, as noted by Dungey et al. (2000), Giese (2008), and Jardet et al. (2010), among others.[6] Work in that tradition, most notably Dungey et al. (2000), finds not only integration but also clear *co*integration, and the common unit roots associated with cointegration imply factor structure.

1.5 Yield Curve Questions

Thus far we have laid the groundwork for subsequent chapters, touching on aspects of yield definition, data construction, and descriptive statistical properties of yields and yield factors. We have emphasized the high

---

[6] Alternatively, more sophisticated models, such as the "square-root process" of Cox et al. (1985), can allow for unit-root dynamics while still enforcing yield nonnegativity by requiring that the conditional variance of yields approach zero as yields approach zero.

persistence of yields, the lesser persistence of yield spreads, and, related, the good empirical approximation afforded by a low-dimensional three-factor structure with highly persistent level and slope factors. Here we roam more widely, in part looking backward, expanding on themes already introduced, and in part looking forward, foreshadowing additional themes that feature prominently in what follows.

1.5.1 Why Use Factor Models for Yields?

The first problem faced in term structure modeling is how to summarize the price information at any point in time for the large number of nominal bonds that are traded. Dynamic factor models prove appealing for three key reasons.

First, as emphasized already, factor structure generally provides a highly accurate empirical description of yield curve data. Because only a small number of systematic risks appear to underlie the pricing of the myriad of tradable financial assets, nearly all bond price information can be summarized with just a few constructed variables or factors. Therefore, yield curve models almost invariably employ a structure that consists of a small set of factors and the associated factor loadings that relate yields of different maturities to those factors.

Second, factor models prove tremendously appealing for statistical reasons. They provide a valuable compression of information, effectively collapsing an intractable high-dimensional modeling situation into a tractable low-dimensional situation. This would be small consolation if the yield data were not well-approximated with factor structure, but again, they are. Hence we're in a most fortunate situation. We *need* low-dimensional factor structure for statistical tractability, and, mercifully, the data actually *have* factor structure.

Related, factor structure is consistent with the "parsimony principle," which we interpret here as the broad insight that imposing restrictions implicitly associated with simple models—even false restrictions that may degrade in-sample fit—often helps to avoid data mining and, related, to produce good out-of-sample forecasts.[7] For example, an unrestricted vector autoregression provides a very general linear model of yields typically with good in-sample fit, but the large number of estimated coefficients may reduce its value for out-of-sample forecasting.[8]

Last, and not at all least, financial economic *theory* suggests, and routinely invokes, factor structure. We see thousands of financial assets in the markets, but for a variety of reasons we view the risk premiums that separate their expected returns as driven by a much smaller number of components, or *risk factors*. In the equity sphere, for example, the celebrated capital asset pricing model (CAPM) is a single-factor model. Various extensions (e.g., Fama and French (1992)) invoke a few additional factors but remain intentionally very low-dimensional, almost always with fewer than five factors. Yield curve factor models are a natural bond market parallel.

1.5.2 How Should Bond Yield Factors and Factor Loadings Be Constructed?

The literature contains a variety of methods for constructing bond yield factors and factor loadings. One

---

[7] See Diebold (2007) for additional discussion.

[8] Parsimony, however, is not the only consideration for determining the number of factors needed; the demands of the precise application are of course also relevant. For example, although just a few factors may account for almost all dynamic yield variation and optimize forecast accuracy, more factors may be needed to fit with great accuracy the cross section of yields at a point in time, say, for pricing derivatives.

approach places structure only on the estimated factors, leaving loadings free. For example, the factors could be the first few principal components, which are restricted to be mutually orthogonal, while the loadings are left unrestricted. Alternatively, the factors could be observed bond portfolios, such as a long-short for slope or a butterfly for curvature.

A second approach, conversely, places structure only on the loadings, leaving factors free. The classic example, which has long been popular among market and central bank practitioners, is the so-called Nelson-Siegel curve, introduced in Nelson and Siegel (1987). As shown by Diebold and Li (2006), a suitably dynamized version of Nelson-Siegel is effectively a dynamic three-factor model of level, slope, and curvature. However, the Nelson-Siegel factors are unobserved, or latent, whereas the associated loadings are restricted by a functional form that imposes smoothness of loadings across maturities, positivity of implied forward rates, and a discount curve that approaches zero with maturity.

A third approach, the no-arbitrage dynamic latent factor model, which is the model of choice in finance, restricts both factors and factor loadings. The most common subclass of such models, affine models in the tradition of Duffie and Kan (1996), postulates linear or affine dynamics for the latent factors and derives the associated restrictions on factor loadings that ensure absence of arbitrage.

1.5.3   Is Imposition of "No-Arbitrage" Useful?

The assumption of no-arbitrage ensures that, after accounting for risk, the dynamic evolution of yields over time is consistent with the cross-sectional shape of the yield curve at any point in time. This consistency condition is likely to hold, given the existence of deep and well-organized bond markets. Hence one might argue that the real markets are at least approximately arbitrage-free, so that a good yield curve model must display freedom from arbitrage.

But all models are false, and subtleties arise once the inevitability of model misspecification is acknowledged. Freedom from arbitrage is essentially an internal consistency condition. But a misspecified model may be internally consistent (free from arbitrage) yet have little relationship to the real world, and hence forecast poorly, for example. Moreover, imposition of no-arbitrage on a misspecified model may actually *degrade* empirical performance.

Conversely, a model may admit arbitrage yet provide a good approximation to a much more complicated reality, and hence forecast well. Moreover, if reality is arbitrage-free, and if a model provides a very good description of reality, then imposition of no-arbitrage would presumably have little effect. That is, an accurate model would be at least approximately arbitrage-free, even if freedom from arbitrage were not explicitly imposed.

Simultaneously, a large literature suggests that coaxing or "shrinking" forecasts in various directions (e.g., reflecting prior views) may improve performance, effectively by producing large reductions in error variance at the cost of only small increases in bias. An obvious benchmark shrinkage direction is toward absence of arbitrage. The key point, however, is that shrinkage methods don't force absence of arbitrage; rather, they coax things *toward* absence of arbitrage.

If we are generally interested in the questions posed in this subsection's title, we are also specifically interested in answering them in the dynamic Nelson-Siegel context.

A first question is whether our dynamic Nelson-Siegel (DNS) model can be made free from arbitrage. A second question, assuming that DNS can be made arbitrage-free, is whether the associated restrictions on the physical yield dynamics improve forecasting performance.

1.5.4 How Should Term Premiums Be Specified?

With risk-neutral investors, yields are equal to the average value of expected future short rates (up to Jensen's inequality terms), and there are no expected excess returns on bonds. In this setting, the expectations hypothesis, which is still a mainstay of much casual and formal macroeconomic analysis, is valid. However, it seems likely that bonds, which provide an uncertain return, are owned by the same risk-averse investors who also demand a large equity premium as compensation for holding risky stocks. Furthermore, as suggested by many statistical tests in the literature, the risk premiums on nominal bonds appear to vary over time, which suggests time-varying risk, time-varying risk aversion, or both (e.g., Campbell and Shiller (1991), Cochrane and Piazzesi (2005)).[9]

In the finance literature, the two basic approaches to modeling time-varying term premiums are time-varying quantities of risk and time-varying "prices of risk" (which translate a unit of factor volatility into a term premium). The large literature on stochastic volatility takes the former approach, allowing the variability of yield factors to change over time. In contrast, the canonical Gaussian affine no-arbitrage finance representation (e.g., Ang

---

[9] However, Diebold et al. (2006b) suggest that the importance of the statistical deviations from the expectations hypothesis may depend on the application.

and Piazzesi (2003)) takes the latter approach, specifying time-varying prices of risk.[10]

1.5.5 How Are Yield Factors and Macroeconomic Variables Related?

The modeling of interest rates has long been a prime example of the disconnect between the macro and finance literatures. In the canonical finance model, the short-term interest rate is a linear function of a few unobserved factors. Movements in long-term yields are importantly determined by changes in risk premiums, which also depend on those latent factors. In contrast, in the macro literature, the short-term interest rate is set by the central bank according to its macroeconomic stabilization goals—such as reducing deviations of inflation and output from the central bank's targets. Furthermore, the macro literature commonly views long-term yields as largely determined by expectations of future short-term interest rates, which in turn depend on expectations of the macro variables; that is, possible changes in risk premiums are often ignored, and the expectations hypothesis of the term structure is employed.

Surprisingly, the disparate finance and macro modeling strategies have long been maintained, largely in isolation of each other. Of course, differences between the finance and macro perspectives reflect, in part, different questions, methods, and avenues of exploration. However, the lack of interchange or overlap between the two research

---

[10]Some recent literature takes an intermediate approach. In a structural dynamic stochastic general equilibrium (DSGE) model, Rudebusch and Swanson (2012) show that technology-type shocks can endogenously generate time-varying prices of risk—namely, conditional heteroskedasticity in the stochastic discount factor—without relying on conditional heteroskedasticity in the driving shocks.

literatures that occurred in the past is striking. Notably, both the DNS and affine no-arbitrage dynamic latent factor models provide useful statistical descriptions of the yield curve, but in their original, most basic, forms they offer little insight into the nature of the underlying economic forces that drive its movements.

Hence, to illuminate the fundamental determinants of interest rates, researchers have begun to incorporate macroeconomic variables into the DNS and affine no-arbitrage dynamic latent factor yield curve models. For example, Diebold et al. (2006b) provide a macroeconomic interpretation of the DNS representation by combining it with vector-autoregressive dynamics for the macroeconomy. Their maximum-likelihood estimation approach extracts 3 latent factors (essentially level, slope, and curvature) from a set of 17 yields on U.S. Treasury securities and simultaneously relates these factors to 3 observable macroeconomic variables (specifically, real activity, inflation, and a monetary policy instrument). By examining the correlations between the DNS yield factors and macroeconomic variables, they find that the level factor is highly correlated with inflation and the slope factor is highly correlated with real activity. The curvature factor appears unrelated to any of the main macroeconomic variables.

The role of macroeconomic variables in a no-arbitrage affine model is explored in several papers. In Ang and Piazzesi (2003), the macroeconomic factors are measures of inflation and real activity, and the joint dynamics of macro factors and additional latent factors are captured by vector autoregressions.[11] They find that output

---

[11] To avoid relying on specific macro series, Ang and Piazzesi construct their measures of real activity and inflation as the first principal component of a large set of candidate macroeconomic series.

shocks have a significant impact on intermediate yields and curvature, while inflation surprises have large effects on the level of the entire yield curve.

For estimation tractability, Ang and Piazzesi allow only for unidirectional dynamics in their arbitrage-free model; specifically, macro variables help determine yields but not the reverse. In contrast, Diebold et al. (2006b) consider a bidirectional characterization of dynamic macro–yield interactions. They find that the causality from the macroeconomy to yields is indeed significantly stronger than in the reverse direction, but that interactions in both directions can be important. Ang et al. (2007) also allow for bidirectional macro-finance links but impose the no-arbitrage restriction as well, which poses a severe estimation challenge. They find that the amount of yield variation that can be attributed to macro factors depends on whether the system allows for bidirectional linkages. When the interactions are constrained to be unidirectional (from macro to yield factors), macro factors can explain only a small portion of the variance of long yields. In contrast, when interactions are allowed to be bidirectional, the system attributes over half of the variance of long yields to macro factors. Similar results in a more robust setting are reported in Bibkov and Chernov (2010).

Finally, Rudebusch and Wu (2008) provide an example of a macro-finance specification that employs more macroeconomic structure and includes both rational expectations and inertial elements. They obtain a good fit to the data with a model that combines an affine no-arbitrage dynamic specification for yields and a small fairly standard macro model, which consists of a monetary policy reaction function, an output Euler equation, and an inflation equation. In their model, the level factor reflects market participants' views about the underlying or medium-term inflation target of the central bank, and the slope factor captures the cyclical response of the central bank, which manipulates the short rate to fulfill its dual mandate to stabilize the real economy and keep inflation close to target. In addition, shocks to the level factor feed back to the real economy through an ex-ante real interest rate.

1.6   Onward

In the chapters that follow, we address the issues and questions raised here, and many others. We introduce DNS in chapter 2, we make it arbitrage-free in chapter 3, and we explore a variety of variations and extensions in chapter 4. In chapter 5 we provide in-depth treatment of aspects of the interplay between the yield curve and the macroeconomy. In chapter 6 we highlight aspects of the current frontier, attempting to separate wheat from chaff, pointing the way toward additional progress.

2

Dynamic Nelson-Siegel

Here we begin our journey. We start with static Nelson-Siegel curve fitting in the cross section, but we proceed quickly to dynamic Nelson-Siegel modeling, with all its nuances and opportunities. Among other things, we emphasize the model's state-space structure, we generalize it to the multicountry context, and we highlight aspects of its use in risk management and forecasting.

2.1 Curve Fitting

As we will see, Nelson-Siegel fits a smooth yield curve to unsmoothed yields. One can arrive at a smooth yield curve in a different way, fitting a smooth discount curve to unsmoothed bond prices and then inferring the implied yield curve. That's how things developed historically, but there are problems, as discussed in Chapter 1.

So let us proceed directly to the static Nelson-Siegel representation. At any time, one sees a large set of yields and may want to fit a smooth curve. Nelson and Siegel (1987) begin with a forward rate curve and fit the function

$$f(\tau) = \beta_1 + \beta_2 e^{-\lambda \tau} + \beta_3 \lambda \tau e^{-\lambda \tau}.$$

The corresponding static Nelson-Siegel yield curve is

$$y(\tau) = \beta_1 + \beta_2 \left(\frac{1 - e^{-\lambda\tau}}{\lambda\tau} \right) + \beta_3 \left(\frac{1 - e^{-\lambda\tau}}{\lambda\tau} - e^{-\lambda\tau} \right).$$

$$(2.1)$$

Note well that these are simply functional form suggestions for fitting the *cross section* of yields.

At first pass, the Nelson-Siegel functional form seems rather arbitrary—a less-than-obvious choice for approximating an arbitrary yield curve. Indeed many other functional forms have been used with some success, perhaps most notably the smoothing splines of Fisher et al. (1995).

But Nelson-Siegel turns out to have some very appealing features. First, it desirably enforces some basic constraints from financial economic theory. For example, the corresponding discount curve satisfies $P(0) = 1$ and $\lim_{\tau \to \infty} P(\tau) = 0$, as appropriate. In addition, the zero-coupon Nelson-Siegel curve satisfies

$$\lim_{\tau \to 0} y(\tau) = f(0) = r,$$

the instantaneous short rate, and $\lim_{\tau \to \infty} y(\tau) = \beta_1$, a constant.

Second, the Nelson-Siegel form provides a parsimonious approximation. Parsimony is desirable because it promotes smoothness (yields tend to be very smooth functions of maturity), it guards against in-sample overfitting (which is important for producing good forecasts), and it promotes empirically tractable and trustworthy estimation (which is always desirable).

Third, despite its parsimony, the Nelson-Siegel form also provides a flexible approximation. Flexibility is desirable because the yield curve assumes a variety of shapes at different times. Inspection reveals that, depending on the values of the four parameters (β_1, β_2, β_3, λ), the Nelson-Siegel curve can be flat, increasing, or decreasing linearly, increasing or decreasing at an increasing or decreasing rate, U-shaped, or upside-down U-shaped. It can't have more than one internal optimum, but that constraint is largely nonbinding, as the yield curve tends not to "wiggle" with maturity.

Fourth, from a mathematical approximation-theoretic viewpoint, the Nelson-Siegel form is far from arbitrary. As Nelson and Siegel insightfully note, the forward rate curve corresponding to the yield curve (2.1) is a constant plus a Laguerre function. Laguerre functions are polynomials multiplied by exponential decay terms and are well-known mathematical approximating functions on the domain $[0, \infty)$, which matches the domain for the term structure. Moreover, as has recently been discovered and as we shall discuss later, the desirable approximation-theoretic properties of Nelson-Siegel go well beyond their Laguerre structure.

For all of these reasons, Nelson-Siegel has become very popular for static curve fitting in practice, particularly among financial market practitioners and central banks, as discussed, for example, in Svensson (1995), BIS (2005), Gürkaynak et al. (2007), and Nyholm (2008). Indeed the Board of Governors of the U.S. Federal Reserve System fits and publishes on the Web daily yield Nelson-Siegel curves in real time, as does the European Central Bank.[1] We now proceed to dynamize the Nelson-Siegel curve.

---

[1] The FRB and ECB curves are actually based on an extension of Nelson-Siegel introduced in Svensson (1995), which we discuss and extend even further in Chapter 4.

2.2   Introducing Dynamics

Following Diebold and Li (2006), let us now recognize
that the Nelson-Siegel parameters must be time-varying
if the yield curve is to be time-varying (as it obviously is).
This leads to a reversal of the perspective associated with
static Nelson-Siegel (2.1), which then produces some key
insights.

2.2.1   Mechanics

Consider a cross-sectional environment for fixed t. The
Nelson-Siegel model is

$$y(\tau) = \beta_1 + \beta_2 \left(\frac{1 - e^{-\lambda\tau}}{\lambda\tau}\right) + \beta_3 \left(\frac{1 - e^{-\lambda\tau}}{\lambda\tau} - e^{-\lambda\tau}\right).$$

This is a cross-sectional linear projection of $y(\tau)$ on variables $(1, ((1 - e^{-\lambda\tau})/\lambda\tau), ((1 - e^{-\lambda\tau})/\lambda\tau - e^{-\lambda\tau}))$ with
parameters β_1, β_2, β_3.[2]

Alternatively, consider a time-series environment for
fixed τ. The model becomes

$$y_t = \beta_{1t} + \beta_{2t} \left(\frac{1 - e^{-\lambda\tau}}{\lambda\tau}\right) + \beta_{3t} \left(\frac{1 - e^{-\lambda\tau}}{\lambda\tau} - e^{-\lambda\tau}\right).$$

This is a time-series linear projection of y_t on *variables*
β_{1t}, β_{2t}, β_{3t} with *parameters* $(1, ((1 - e^{-\lambda\tau})/\lambda\tau), ((1 - e^{-\lambda\tau})/\lambda\tau - e^{-\lambda\tau}))$.

Hence from a cross-sectional perspective the βs are
parameters, but from a time-series perspective the βs
are variables. Combining the spatial and temporal perspectives produces the *dynamic Nelson-Siegel (DNS)
model*:

$$y_t(\tau) = \beta_{1t} + \beta_{2t} \left(\frac{1 - e^{-\lambda\tau}}{\lambda\tau}\right) + \beta_{3t} \left(\frac{1 - e^{-\lambda\tau}}{\lambda\tau} - e^{-\lambda\tau}\right).$$

$$(2.2)$$

---

[2]For now, assume that λ is known. We will elaborate on λ later.

Much of this book is concerned with the DNS model (2.2) and its many variations, extensions, and uses.

2.2.2 Interpretation

Operationally, the DNS model (2.2) is nothing more than the Nelson-Siegel model (2.1) with time-varying parameters. The interpretation, however, is deep: DNS distills the yield curve into three dynamic, latent factors (β_{1t}, β_{2t}, and β_{3t}), the dynamics of which determine entirely the dynamics of y_t for any τ, and the coefficients ("factor loadings") of which determine entirely the cross section of $y(\tau)$ for any t.

DNS is a leading example of a "dynamic factor model," in which a high-dimensional set of variables (in this case, the many yields across maturities) is actually driven by much lower-dimensional state dynamics (in this case the three latent yield factors). Dynamic factor models trace to Sargent and Sims (1977) and Geweke (1977).[3]

Dynamic factor structure is very convenient statistically, as it converts seemingly intractable high-dimensional situations into easily handled low-dimensional situations. Of course, if one simply *assumed* factor structure but the data did not satisfy it, one would simply have a misspecified model. Fortunately, however, financial asset returns typically *do* display low-dimensional factor structure. The dozens of bond yields that we see, to take an example close to our interests, clearly are not evolving independently. Instead they tend to move together, not in lockstep of course, as multiple factors are at work, as are idiosyncratic factors, which we will see shortly when we enrich the model. The same is true for stock and foreign exchange markets, as well as for macroeconomic fundamentals, which move together over the business cycle.

---

[3] See also Watson and Engle (1983).

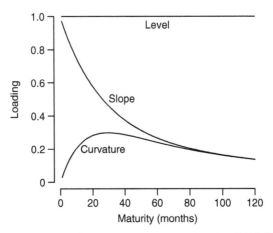

Figure 2.1. DNS Factor Loadings. We plot DNS factor loadings as a function of maturity, for $\lambda = 0.0609$.

For this reason, factor structure is now central to the theory and practice of financial asset pricing.[4]

One naturally wants to understand more about the latent factors β_{1t}, β_{2t}, and β_{3t}. Just what *are* they? What do they *do*? The answer follows from inspection of the factor loadings, which we plot as a function of maturity in Figure 2.1.

First consider the loading on β_{2t}, $(1 - e^{-\lambda\tau})/\lambda\tau$, a function that starts at 1 but decays monotonically and quickly to 0. Hence it was often called a "short-term factor," mostly affecting short-term yields.

Next consider the loading on β_{3t}, $(1 - e^{-\lambda\tau})/\lambda\tau - e^{-\lambda\tau}$, which starts at 0 (and is thus not short term), increases, and then decays to zero (and thus is not long term). Hence it was often called a "medium-term factor," mostly affecting medium-term yields.

---

[4] See, for example, Campbell et al. (1997) and Cochrane (2001).

Finally, consider the loading on β_{1t}, which is constant at 1, and so not decaying to zero in the limit. Hence, unlike the other two factors, it affects long yields and therefore was often called a "long-term factor."

Thus far we have called the three factors long term, short term, and medium term, in reference to the yield maturities at which they have maximal respective relative impact. Note, however, that they may also be interpreted in terms of their effect on the *overall yield curve shape*. Immediately, for example, β_{1t} governs the yield curve *level*: An increase in β_{1t} shifts the curve in parallel fashion, increasing all yields equally, as the loading on β_{1t} is identical at all maturities. Similarly, β_{2t} governs the yield curve *slope*: An increase in β_{2t} increases short yields substantially (they load heavily on β_{2t}) but leaves long yields unchanged (they load negligibly on β_{2t}).[5] Finally, β_{3t} governs the yield curve *curvature*: An increase in β_{3t} doesn't change short yields much (they don't load much on β_{3t}) and doesn't change long yields much (they too don't load much on β_{3t}), but it changes medium-maturity yields (they load relatively heavily on β_{3t}).

If β_{1t} governs the level of the yield curve and β_{2t} governs its slope, it is interesting to note, moreover, that the instantaneous yield depends on *both* the level and slope factors, because $y_t(0) = \beta_{1t} + \beta_{2t}$. Several other models have the same implication. In particular, Dai and Singleton (2000) show that the three-factor models of Balduzzi et al. (1996) and Chen (1996) impose the restriction that the instantaneous yield is an affine function of only two of the three state variables, a property

---

[5] It is interesting to note that some authors, such as Frankel and Lown (1994), define the yield curve slope as $y_t(0) - y_t(\infty)$, which is *exactly* equal to β_{2t}.

shared by the three-factor nonaffine model of Andersen and Lund (1997).

2.2.3 Alternative Factorizations

We are now in a position to note that what we have called the "Nelson-Siegel curve" is actually a different factorization than the one originally advocated by Nelson and Siegel (1987), who used

$$y_t(\tau) = b_{1t} + b_{2t}\left(\frac{1 - e^{-\lambda\tau}}{\lambda\tau}\right) - b_{3t}\left(e^{-\lambda\tau}\right).$$

The original Nelson-Siegel yield curve matches ours with $b_{1t} = \beta_{1t}$, $b_{2t} = \beta_{2t} + \beta_{3t}$, and $b_{3t} = \beta_{3t}$. In the Nelson-Siegel factorization, however, the loadings $(1 - e^{-\lambda\tau})/\lambda\tau$ and $e^{-\lambda\tau}$ have similar monotonically decreasing shape, which makes it hard to give different interpretations to the different factors b_{2t} and b_{3t}. In our factorization, the loadings have distinctly different shapes and the factors have corresponding distinctly different interpretations as level, slope, and curvature.

2.3 State-Space Representation

Changing to a notation that emphasizes the "level, slope, curvature" interpretation of the DNS factors, we write the DNS model as

$$y_t(\tau) = l_t + s_t\left(\frac{1 - e^{-\lambda\tau}}{\lambda\tau}\right) + c_t\left(\frac{1 - e^{-\lambda\tau}}{\lambda\tau} - e^{-\lambda\tau}\right),$$

$t = 1, \ldots, T$, $\tau = 1, \ldots, N$. Following Diebold et al. (2006b), we also now move to a state-space interpretation.

2.3.1 Measurement and Transition

Adding stochastic error terms to the deterministic DNS curve produces the measurement equation, which stochastically relates the set of N yields to the three unobservable yield factors,

$$y_t = \Lambda f_t + \varepsilon_t, \qquad (2.3)$$

where the variables are

$$y_t = \begin{pmatrix} y_t(\tau_1) \\ y_t(\tau_2) \\ \vdots \\ y_t(\tau_N) \end{pmatrix}, \qquad f_t = \begin{pmatrix} l_t \\ s_t \\ c_t \end{pmatrix}, \qquad \varepsilon_t = \begin{pmatrix} \varepsilon_t(\tau_1) \\ \varepsilon_t(\tau_2) \\ \vdots \\ \varepsilon_t(\tau_N) \end{pmatrix}$$

and the parameter matrix is

$$\Lambda = \begin{pmatrix} 1 & \dfrac{1 - e^{-\tau_1 \lambda}}{\tau_1 \lambda} & \dfrac{1 - e^{-\tau_1 \lambda}}{\tau_1 \lambda} - e^{-\tau_1 \lambda} \\ 1 & \dfrac{1 - e^{-\tau_2 \lambda}}{\tau_2 \lambda} & \dfrac{1 - e^{-\tau_2 \lambda}}{\tau_2 \lambda} - e^{-\tau_2 \lambda} \\ \vdots & \vdots & \vdots \\ 1 & \dfrac{1 - e^{-\tau_N \lambda}}{\tau_N \lambda} & \dfrac{1 - e^{-\tau_N \lambda}}{\tau_N \lambda} - e^{-\tau_N \lambda} \end{pmatrix},$$

$t = 1, \ldots, T$. We interpret the stochastic errors $\varepsilon_t(\tau)$ as "idiosyncratic," or maturity-specific, factors. Hence each yield $y_t(\tau)$ is driven in part by the common factors l_t, s_t, and c_t (which is why the yield movements cohere in certain ways) and in part by its idiosyncratic factor $\varepsilon_t(\tau)$.

Now we need to specify the common factor dynamics, that is, the transition equation. We use a first-order vector autoregression,

$$(f_t - \mu) = A(f_{t-1} - \mu) + \eta_t, \qquad (2.4)$$

where the variables are

$$f_t = \begin{pmatrix} l_t \\ s_t \\ c_t \end{pmatrix}, \qquad \eta_t = \begin{pmatrix} \eta_t^l \\ \eta_t^s \\ \eta_t^c \end{pmatrix}$$

and the parameter vectors and matrices are

$$\mu = \begin{pmatrix} \mu^l \\ \mu^s \\ \mu^c \end{pmatrix}, \qquad A = \begin{pmatrix} a_{11} & a_{12} & a_{13} \\ a_{21} & a_{22} & a_{23} \\ a_{31} & a_{32} & a_{33} \end{pmatrix}.$$

Obviously, μ is the factor mean and A governs the factor dynamics.

The state-space framework is extremely general. For notational convenience we write the state dynamics as first-order in the yield factors, but as is well-known, higher-order dynamics can always be rewritten as a first-order system. Hence the state-space framework includes as special cases almost any linear dynamics imaginable.[6] See Golinski and Zaffaroni (2011) for interesting applications of long-memory ideas in DNS yield curve modeling.

To complete the system we now have only to specify the covariance structure of the measurement and transition disturbances. We make the standard assumptions that the white noise transition and measurement disturbances are orthogonal to each other and to the initial

---

[6] One exception—perhaps the only exception of interest—is long-memory dynamics, which do not admit representation with finite-dimensional state. Long-memory processes can, however, be approximated arbitrarily well by sums of simple first-order autoregressions, as shown by Granger (1980).

state:

$$\begin{pmatrix} \eta_t \\ \varepsilon_t \end{pmatrix} \sim WN \left(\begin{pmatrix} 0 \\ 0 \end{pmatrix} \begin{pmatrix} Q & 0 \\ 0 & H \end{pmatrix} \right), \tag{2.5}$$

$$E(f_0 \eta_t') = 0, \tag{2.6}$$
$$E(f_0 \varepsilon_t') = 0.$$

Note that we have not assumed Gaussian measurement and/or transition disturbances. Normality is not required for what follows, although the efficiency properties of various extractions, forecasts, and estimators based on the system (2.3)–(2.6) will differ depending on whether normality is satisfied.

The state-space representation (2.3)–(2.6) is of course not unique. Instead of centering the state vector around a nonzero mean, for example, we could have simply included a constant in either the measurement or transition equation. Such choices are generally inconsequential. However, a deeper issue of identification in factor models typically requires that one normalize either a common factor loading or an idiosyncratic factor variance.

2.3.2 Optimal Extractions and Predictions

The DNS state-space structure implies that the Kalman filter is immediately applicable for optimal filtering and smoothing of the latent yield factors (in an obvious notation, $f_{t,1:t}$ and $f_{t,1:T}$), as well as for optimal one-step-ahead or general h-step-ahead prediction of both the yield factors and the observed yields ($f_{t+1,1:t}$, $f_{t+h,1:t}$, $y_{t+1,1:t}$, $y_{t+h,1:t}$). The optimality of Kalman filter extractions and predictions is in the linear least squares sense. Hence under normality the Kalman filter delivers conditional expectations, whereas more generally it delivers linear projections. These results, and the mechanics of

implementing them, are standard.[7] Filtering, smoothing,
and prediction are of course conditional on a particular
set of parameter values. In practice the parameters are
unknown and must be estimated, to which we now turn.

2.4   Estimation

Several procedures are available for estimating the DNS
model, ranging from a simple two-step procedure, to
exact maximum likelihood estimation using the state-
space representation in conjunction with the Kalman
filter, to Bayesian analysis using Markov-chain Monte
Carlo methods. We now introduce them and provide
some comparative assessment.

2.4.1   Static Nelson-Siegel in Cross Section

First consider estimation of the static Nelson-Siegel
model in the cross section. The four-parameter Nelson-
Siegel curve (2.1) is intrinsically nonlinear but may be
estimated by iterative numerical minimization of the
sum of squares function (nonlinear least squares). Importantly, moreover, note that if λ is known or can be
calibrated, estimation involves just trivial *linear* least
squares regression of $y(\tau)$ on 1, $((1 - e^{-\lambda\tau})/\lambda\tau)$, and
$((1 - e^{-\lambda\tau})/\lambda\tau - e^{-\lambda\tau})$.

   In practice λ *can* often be credibly calibrated and
treated as known, as follows. Note that λ determines
where the loading on the curvature factor c_t achieves its
maximum. For c_t to drive curvature, its loading should
be maximal at a medium maturity τ_m. One can simply
choose a reasonable τ_m and reverse engineer the corresponding λ_m. Values of m in the range of two or three

---

[7] For details see standard texts such as Harvey (1990).

years are commonly used; for example, Diebold and Li (2006) use $m = 30$ months. Model fit is typically robust to the precise choice of λ.

2.4.2 Two-Step DNS

The first estimation approach, so-called two-step DNS, was introduced by Diebold and Li (2006). Consider first the case of calibrated λ. In step 1, we fit the static Nelson-Siegel model (2.1) for each period $t = 1, \ldots, T$ by OLS. This yields a three-dimensional time series of estimated factors, $\{\hat{l}_t, \hat{s}_t, \hat{c}_t\}_{t=1}^{T}$, and a corresponding N-dimensional series of residual pricing errors ("measurement disturbances"), $\{\hat{\varepsilon}_t(\tau_1), \hat{\varepsilon}_t(\tau_2), \hat{\varepsilon}_t(\tau_N)\}_{t=1}^{T}$.[8] The key is that DNS distills an N-dimensional time series of yields into a three-dimensional time series of yield factors, $\{\hat{l}_t, \hat{s}_t, \hat{c}_t\}_{t=1}^{T}$.

Next, in step 2, we fit a dynamic model to $\{\hat{l}_t, \hat{s}_t, \hat{c}_t\}_{t=1}^{T}$. An obvious choice is a vector autoregression, but there are many possible variations, some of which we will discuss subsequently. Step 2 yields estimates of dynamic parameters governing the evolution of the yield factors ("transition equation parameters"), as well as estimates of the factor innovations ("transition disturbances").

The benefits of two-step estimation with calibrated λ (relative to one-step estimation, which we will discuss shortly) are its simplicity, convenience, and numerical stability: Nothing is required but trivial linear

---

[8] Note that because the maturities are not equally spaced, we implicitly weight the most "active" region of the yield curve most heavily when fitting the model, which seems desirable. It would be interesting to explore loss functions that go even further in reflecting such economic considerations, based, for example, on bond portfolio pricing or success of trading rules, such as that done in different but related contexts by Bates (1999) and Fabozzi et al. (2005). Thus far, the DNS literature has not pursued that route aggressively.

regressions. Moreover, one can of course estimate λ as well, if desired, with only a slight increase in complication. The first-step OLS regressions then become four-parameter nonlinear least squares regressions, and the second-step three-dimensional dynamic model for $\{\hat{l}_t, \hat{s}_t, \hat{c}_t\}_{t=1}^{T}$ becomes a four-dimensional dynamic model for $\{\hat{l}_t, \hat{s}_t, \hat{c}_t, \hat{\lambda}_t\}_{t=1}^{T}.$[9] The cost of two-step estimation is its possible statistical suboptimality, insofar as the first-step parameter estimation error is ignored in the second step, which may distort second-step inference.

2.4.3   One-Step DNS

The second estimation approach, which was introduced by Diebold et al. (2006b), is so-called one-step DNS. The basic insight is that exploitation to the state-space structure of DNS allows one to do all estimation simultaneously.

One-step estimation can be approached and achieved in several ways. On the classical side, exact maximum-likelihood estimation may be done using the Kalman filter, which delivers the innovations needed for evaluation of the Gaussian pseudo likelihood, which can be maximized using traditional (e.g., gradient-based) numerical methods. Alternatively, still using the Kalman filter, one can find the likelihood maximum using data-augmentation methods such as the expectation maximization (EM) algorithm. Finally, if one is willing and able to specify prior distributions for all coefficients, one

---

[9] Note that we have thus far considered two rather extreme cases for λ: calibrated and fixed, or estimated and time-varying. One might of course be interested in the intermediate case of λ estimated but fixed. This turns out to be challenging with two-step estimation, but simple with the one-step estimation introduced later.

can again exploit the state-space structure of DNS to do a full Bayesian analysis.[10]

2.4.3.1 Numerical Gaussian QMLE

As is well-known, running the Kalman filter on the state-space representation of our model (2.3)–(2.4) delivers the one-step-ahead prediction errors with which the Gaussian pseudo likelihood can be evaluated for any parameter configuration. One may then find numerically the parameter configuration that maximizes the likelihood. Traditional gradient-based optimization methods, as used, for example, in Diebold et al. (2006b), are historically the most popular approach, and refinements such as the analytic score functions provided by Koopman and Shephard (1992) can be incorporated to improve performance.

However, the N-yield system (2.3)–(2.6) has many parameters. The measurement equation (2.3) has no parameters with fixed λ, and one parameter with estimated λ. The transition equation (2.4), however, has 12 parameters (three means and nine dynamic parameters). And, crucially, the measurement and transition disturbances have rich variance-covariance structure (2.5). The measurement disturbance covariance matrix has $(N^2 + N)/2$ parameters, and the transition disturbance covariance matrix has six parameters.

This is a large number of parameters to estimate credibly by traditional gradient-based numerical optimization methods. A typical system with 15 yields, for example, has 139 parameters. Even a potentially draconian assumption like diagonal A, Q, and H matrices still

---

[10] For algorithmic detail regarding Bayesian analysis of state-space models, see, for example, Koop (2003). Here we stress issues and intuition.

leaves $N + 10$ parameters, a challenging if not absurd situation (and of course one does not generally *want* to assume such diagonality).

The upshot: QMLE by traditional gradient-based numerical likelihood maximization is often intractable and challenging at best. Another approach replaces traditional gradient-based optimization calculations with a sequence of linear operations that takes one to the same place. The EM algorithm, to which we now turn, does precisely that.

2.4.3.2   The EM algorithm for Gaussian QMLE

The simple and compelling EM algorithm is tailor-made for state-space models, exploiting the insight that if the parameters are known, then it's easy to make a good guess of the state sequence, and conversely, if the state sequence is known, then it's easy to construct a good estimate of the parameters. The EM algorithm converts likelihood maximization into an iterative sequence of state extractions and linear regressions, and it is guaranteed to increase the likelihood at each iteration.[11]

The intuition of the EM algorithm is strong. Imagine that we somehow *know* the state vector, $\{l_t, s_t, c_t\}_{t=1}^T$. Then parameter estimation is straightforward; estimation of the measurement equation (2.3) is just estimation of a seemingly unrelated regression system, and estimation of the transition equation (2.4) is just estimation of a first-order vector autoregression, both of which are standard, stable, and fast.

---

[11] See Tanner (1993) for a more detailed discussion of EM, related methods, and relevant references. The classic econometric implementation of EM in dynamic factor models is Watson and Engle (1983), and Reis and Watson (2010) provide a recent econometric application in a high-dimensional situation.

In reality, of course, we don't know the state vector, but for any given parameter configuration we can extract it optimally using the Kalman filter. (That's roughly the E step.) Then, conditional on that extracted state vector, we can run the seemingly unrelated regression and vector autoregression above and get new, updated parameter estimates. (That's roughly the M step.) Then, using the updated parameter estimates we can get an updated state vector extraction, and so forth, continuing iteratively until convergence.

Note that the two-step DNS estimator is very similar to one iteration of EM. In two-step DNS we run one set of regressions (one time) to estimate the state vector, and then conditional on that estimated state vector we run another set of regressions (one time) to estimate the system parameters.

2.4.3.3 *Fast filtering for Gaussian QMLE*

Perhaps surprisingly, although high-dimensional parameter spaces always present challenges, the high-dimensional observed vector of yields also presents problems regardless of the number of underlying parameters, because it makes for slow Kalman filtering and smoothing. Hence slow filtering affects both the gradient-based optimization of section 2.4.3.1 and the EM-based optimization of section 2.4.3.2.

Jungbacker and Koopman (2008), however, show how to achieve fast filtering. They show that dynamic factor models may generally be transformed such that the observed vector is of the same dimension as the state vector. Their approach, together with the efficient multivariate filtering methods of Koopman and Durbin (2000) and the earlier-mentioned analytic score function of Koopman and Shephard (1992), helps deliver practical gradient-based numerical Gaussian QMLE.

Alternatively, as discussed earlier, one can dispense with gradient methods and use EM instead. The Jungbacker and Koopman (2008) and Koopman and Durbin (2000) results are equally useful in that context, however, because it still requires many runs of the Kalman filter.

Finally, one can often blend the methods productively. Two-step DNS, for example, may provide quick and accurate startup values for EM iteration. The EM algorithm, moreover, typically gets close to an optimum very quickly but is ultimately slow to reach full convergence.[12] Hence one may then switch to a gradient-based method, which can quickly move to an optimum when given highly accurate startup values from EM.

2.4.3.4 Bayesian estimation

Optimization in high-dimensional spaces is always a challenging problem. Some of the methods or combinations of methods discussed thus far may confront that problem better than others, but all must nevertheless grapple with it.

Moving to a Bayesian approach may therefore be helpful, because it replaces optimization with *averaging* in the estimation of moments (e.g., posterior means). Averaging is mathematically easier than optimization.[13]

Quite apart from the pragmatic motivation above, Bayesian analysis of DNS may also be intrinsically appealing for the usual reasons (see, for example, Koop (2003)) as long as one is willing and able to specify a credible prior and likelihood. The multimove Gibbs

---

[12] In the original EM paper, Dempster et al. (1977) show that EM converges at a linear rate, in contrast to the faster quadratic rate achieved by many gradient-based algorithms.

[13] Optimization and averaging are of course related, however, as emphasized by Chernozhukov and Hong (2003).

sampler of Carter and Kohn (1994) facilitates simple Bayesian analysis of state-space models such as DNS.[14]

In addition, Bayesian analysis may be especially appealing in the DNS context because there is a potentially natural shrinkage direction (i.e., a natural prior mean), corresponding to the restrictions associated with the absence of arbitrage possibilities. We shall subsequently have much to say about absence of arbitrage, what it implies in the DNS context, and whether its strict imposition is desirable. Bayesian shrinkage estimation is potentially appealing because it blends prior and data information, coaxing but not forcing the MLE toward the prior mean, with the exact amount depending on prior precision versus likelihood curvature. In any event, if one is going to shrink the maximum-likelihood estimates in one direction or another, a natural shrinkage direction—and one clearly motivated by financial economic theory—would appear to be toward no-arbitrage.

2.4.3.5 Discussion

In our view, there is no doubt that the state-space framework is a powerful and productive way to conceptualize the structure and estimation of DNS. There is also little doubt that the one-step estimation afforded by the state-space framework is superior to two-step estimation in principle.

We conjecture, however, that little is lost in practice by using two-step estimation, because there is typically enough cross-sectional variation such that $\hat{l}_t$, $\hat{s}_t$, and $\hat{c}_t$ are estimated very precisely at each time t. Moreover, in applications we have found that gradient-based

---

[14] See also the exposition and insightful applications in Kim and Nelson (1999).

one-step estimation is frequently intractable or incompletely trustworthy. In particular, if forced to choose between two-step and traditional gradient-based one-step estimation procedures, we would lean toward the two-step method. When traditional one-step converges, two-step nevertheless tends to match closely, but one-step doesn't always converge in a trustworthy fashion, whereas two-step is always simple and trustworthy.[15]

The EM and Bayesian one-step methods that we sketched above, however, are in certain respects much more sophisticated and more numerically stable than traditional gradient-based one-step methods. Bayesian Markov-chain Monte Carlo methods are, after all, now frequently and successfully employed in modeling environments with many hundreds of parameters, and there is no obvious reason why DNS should be an exception. Hence it will be interesting to see how the literature develops as experience accumulates, and which estimation approach is ultimately preferred.

2.5 Multicountry Modeling

The state-space structure of DNS makes it easy to generalize to incorporate a layered, hierarchical structure. This is useful for modeling sets of yield curves, which arise naturally in multicountry analyses in which country yields can depend on country factors, and country

---

[15] In addition, within the two-step estimation paradigm one could use the methods of Pagan (1984) to formally address the "generated regressor" problem, possibly enhancing the reliability of second-step standard errors. To the best of our knowledge, the DNS literature thus far has featured neither a comparison of one-step vs. two-step estimation nor a comparison of two-step estimation vs. "generated regressor adjusted" two-step estimation.

factors can depend on *global* factors, as in Diebold et al. (2008).[16]

2.5.1 Global Yields

Imagine a set of "global yields," each of which depends on latent global common level, slope, and curvature factors and a global idiosyncratic factor,

$$Y_t(\tau) = L_t + S_t \left(\frac{1 - e^{-\lambda\tau}}{\lambda\tau} \right)$$
$$+ C_t \left(\frac{1 - e^{-\lambda\tau}}{\lambda\tau} - e^{-\lambda\tau} \right) + E_t(\tau), \quad (2.7)$$

where the $Y_t(\tau)$ are global yields, L_t, S_t, and C_t are global common factors, and E_t is a global idiosyncratic factor.

We endow the global common factors with simple autoregressive dynamics,

$$\begin{pmatrix} L_t \\ S_t \\ C_t \end{pmatrix} = \begin{pmatrix} \Phi_{11} & \Phi_{12} & \Phi_{13} \\ \Phi_{21} & \Phi_{22} & \Phi_{23} \\ \Phi_{31} & \Phi_{32} & \Phi_{33} \end{pmatrix} \begin{pmatrix} L_{t-1} \\ S_{t-1} \\ C_{t-1} \end{pmatrix} + \begin{pmatrix} U_t^L \\ U_t^S \\ U_t^C \end{pmatrix}, \quad (2.8)$$

where U_t^L, U_t^S, and U_t^C are global state transition shocks, or, in a more concise notation that we will use later,

$$F_t = \Phi F_{t-1} + U_t, \quad (2.9)$$

where $F_t = (L_t, S_t, C_t)'$ and $U_t = (U_t^L, U_t^S, U_t^C)'$.

One might wonder what, precisely, are "global yields," and from where we obtain data for them. It turns out that we don't need data for them, as we will soon show.

---

[16] Similar structures have been used effectively in the macroeconometric literature on global business cycle modeling, including Gregory et al. (1997), Kose et al. (2008), and Aruoba et al. (2011).

2.5.2 Country Yields

In a multicountry layered factor framework, each country's yield curve remains characterized as in standard DNS,

$$y_{it}(\tau) = l_{it} + s_{it}\left(\frac{1 - e^{-\lambda\tau}}{\lambda\tau}\right)$$
$$+ c_{it}\left(\frac{1 - e^{-\lambda\tau}}{\lambda\tau} - e^{-\lambda\tau}\right) + \varepsilon_{it}(\tau), \quad (2.10)$$

where l_{it}, s_{it}, and c_{it} are latent level, slope, and curvature country common factors and ε_{it} is a country idiosyncratic factor.[17]

Now, however, the country common factors l_{it}, s_{it}, and c_{it} load on the global common factors L_t, S_t, and C_t, respectively:

$$l_{it} = \alpha_i^l + \beta_i^l L_t + \eta_{it}^l, \quad (2.11)$$
$$s_{it} = \alpha_i^s + \beta_i^s S_t + \eta_{it}^s, \quad (2.12)$$
$$c_{it} = \alpha_i^c + \beta_i^c C_t + \eta_{it}^c, \quad (2.13)$$

where α_i^l, α_i^s, and α_i^c are constant terms, β_i^l, β_i^s, and β_i^c are loadings on global common factors, and η_{it}^l, η_{it}^s, and η_{it}^c are zero-mean stochastic disturbances.

2.5.3 State-Space Representation

Stacking across maturities and countries, the transition equation remains (2.9), which we repeat for convenience:

$$F_t = \Phi F_{t-1} + U_t.$$

The measurement equation (in an obvious notation) is

$$y_t = \Lambda(A + BF_t + \eta_t) + \varepsilon_t$$
$$= (\Lambda A) + (\Lambda B)F_t + (\Lambda\eta_t + \varepsilon_t),$$

---

[17] Note that we have fixed λ over both time and space. It might be interesting to relax that assumption.

where y_t contains yields (for all countries and maturities), Λ contains the DNS factor loadings (for all maturities), A contains the intercepts in the equations relating country factors to global factors (for all countries and country factors), B contains the slopes in the equations relating country factors to global factors (for all countries and country factors), η_t contains the stochastic shocks in the equations relating country factors to global factors (for all countries and country factors), and ε_t contains the yield curve stochastic shocks (for all countries and maturities).

2.5.4 Discussion

Note that we do not require observation of global yields or global yield factors. Global yields $Y_t(\tau)$ do not appear at all in the state-space representation, the measurement equation of which instead relates observed *country* yields to the latent global yield *factors* L_t, S_t, and C_t, which appear in the state vector. Once the model is estimated, L_t, S_t, and C_t can be extracted using the Kalman smoother.

A variety of assumptions are possible regarding the serial correlation and cross-correlation structures of the various shocks (and indeed whether and where the shocks appear). Thus far, we have been deliberately vague to avoid locking ourselves into any particular special case. Simplest is to assume that all shocks are white noise, orthogonal to all other shocks at all leads and lags. But one could easily imagine wanting more flexibility, for example, through serially correlated η shocks, which would allow for country common factor dynamics other than those inherited from the global common factors.

Many approaches to identification are also possible. The issue of identifying restrictions is related to the issue of stochastic assumptions. In many cases the traditional approaches of normalizing selected factor loadings and/or variances will suffice, but the details necessarily depend on the specific model adopted.

Quite apart from technical issues of statistical flexibility and parameter identification, interesting economic extensions of the basic model (2.7)–(2.13) are also possible. For example, one could allow for more layers in the hierarchical factor structure. Country factors, for example, might depend on *regional* factors (e.g., Europe, Asia), which then might depend on global factors.

2.6   Risk Management

The standard bond portfolio risk measure, duration, measures the sensitivity of bond portfolio value to interest rate changes. In multifactor environments, however, the well-known Macaulay duration (e.g., Campbell et al. (1997)) is an inadequate measure of bond portfolio risk, because it accounts only for *level* shifts in the yield curve. That is, it is effectively based on a one-factor model.

Hence authors such as Chambers et al. (1988), Willner (1996) and Diebold et al. (2006a) propose generalized duration measures, or so-called duration vectors.[18] Each element of a duration vector captures bond price sensitivity to a particular factor. The three-factor DNS model immediately suggests generalized duration components corresponding not only to level, but also to slope and curvature.

In general we can define a bond duration measure as follows. Let the cash flows from the bond be $C_1, C_2, \ldots,$

---

[18] See also Garbade (1999).

C_I, and let the associated times to maturity be $\tau_1, \tau_2,$
$\ldots, \tau_I$. Assume also that the zero-coupon yield curve is
linear in a set of arbitrary factors. In keeping with our
DNS perspective we assume three factors, f_1, f_2, and f_3,
but of course more could be added. We write

$$y_t(\tau) = B_1(\tau)f_{1t} + B_2(\tau)f_{2t} + B_3(\tau)f_{3t}, \qquad (2.14)$$
$$dy_t(\tau) = B_1(\tau)df_{1t} + B_2(\tau)df_{2t} + B_3(\tau)df_{3t}.$$

Then, assuming continuous compounding, the price of
the bond is

$$P = \sum_{i=1}^{I} C_i e^{-\tau_i y_t(\tau_i)},$$

where we discount cash flow C_i using the corresponding zero-coupon yield $y_t(\tau_i)$. For an arbitrary yield curve
movement, the price change is

$$dP = \sum_{i=1}^{I} \left(\frac{\partial P}{\partial y_t(\tau_i)} \right) dy_t(\tau_i)$$

$$= \sum_{i=1}^{I} \left(C_i e^{-\tau_i y_t(\tau_i)}(-\tau_i) \right) dy_t(\tau_i),$$

where we have treated $y_t(\tau_i)$ as independent variables.
Therefore

$$-\frac{dP}{P} = \sum_{i=1}^{I} \left(\frac{1}{P} C_i e^{-\tau_i y_t(\tau_i)} \tau_i \right) dy_t(\tau_i)$$

$$= \sum_{i=1}^{I} \left(\frac{1}{P} C_i e^{-\tau_i y_t(\tau_i)} \tau_i \right) \sum_{j=1}^{3} B_j(\tau_i) df_{jt},$$

where we have used (2.14) to produce the second equal-
ity. Rearranging terms, we can express the percentage

change in bond price as a function of changes in the factors

$$-\frac{dP}{P} = \sum_{j=1}^{3} \left\{ \sum_{i=1}^{I} \left[\frac{1}{P} C_i e^{-\tau_i y(\tau_i)} \tau_i \right] B_j(\tau_i) \right\} df_{jt} \quad (2.15)$$

$$= \sum_{j=1}^{3} \left\{ \sum_{i=1}^{I} w_i \tau_i B_j(\tau_i) \right\} df_{jt},$$

where w_i is the weight associated with C_i.

In (2.15), we decomposed the bond price change into changes coming from different risk factors. Hence we can define the duration component associated with each risk factor as

$$D_j = \sum_{i=1}^{I} w_i \tau_i B_j(\tau_i); \quad j = 1, 2, 3.$$

In particular, the duration vector of any coupon bond, based on the three-factor DNS model, is

$$D_1 = \sum_{i=1}^{I} w_i \tau_i,$$

$$D_2 = \sum_{i=1}^{I} w_i \frac{1 - e^{-\lambda \tau_i}}{\lambda},$$

$$D_3 = \sum_{i=1}^{I} w_i \left(\frac{1 - e^{-\lambda \tau_i}}{\lambda} - \tau_i e^{-\lambda \tau_i} \right).$$

Note that the first element of the duration vector is exactly the traditional Macaulay duration, while the second and third elements capture response to nonlevel (i.e., slope and curvature) shifts.[19]

Verifying that the elements of the DNS duration vector increase with τ, decrease with the coupon rate, and decrease with the yield to maturity is straightforward. In addition, they have the "portfolio property": a bond portfolio's D_j is a weighted average of its component bonds' D_j's, where the weights assigned to the component bonds are their shares in portfolio value.

2.7 DNS Fit and Forecasting

There are by now literally hundreds of DNS applications involving model fitting and forecasting. The original paper of Diebold and Li (2006) finds good fits and forecasts for a certain sample of U.S. government bond yields, but subsequent empirical results of course vary across studies that involve different sample periods, different sets of yields, different countries, and so forth. For example, Mönch (2008) finds that the clear superiority of DNS found in Diebold and Li (2006) is not confirmed on a certain set of subsequent U.S. data, whereas Alper et al. (2007) find good forecasting performance for another country (Turkey). Nevertheless, all told, DNS tends to fit and forecast well, which, combined with its simplicity, is responsible for its popularity. Here we elaborate.

First consider DNS fits. Nelson-Siegel and related three-factor models of level, slope, and curvature have been observed to fit well in the cross section for several decades, from the original work of Nelson and Siegel

---

[19] DNS-based vector duration, with its good properties asymptotically in τ, contrasts to the closely related polynomial-based vector duration proposed by Chambers et al. (1988), $D_1' = \sum_{i=1}^{I} w_i \tau_i$, $D_2' = \sum_{i=1}^{I} (w_i \tau_i^2)^{1/2}$, and $D_3' = \sum_{i=1}^{I} (w_i \tau_i^3)^{1/3}$, which suffers from the bad properties of polynomials asymptotically in τ.

(1987) through the ongoing fits of Gürkaynak et al. (2007), written to the Web daily by the U.S. Federal Reserve.[20]

Good cross-sectional fit is not too surprising, because Nelson-Siegel is actually quite a flexible functional form. Nelson-Siegel curves are smooth, and real yield curves tend to be smooth. They can have at most one internal optimum, but that restriction is rarely violated in the data. They can be flat, increasing or decreasing at increasing, decreasing, or constant rates. Of course they don't fit observed yields *exactly*, but from a predictive viewpoint that's natural and desirable, as their tightly parametric structure guards against in-sample overfitting.

Now consider the fit of *dynamic* Nelson-Siegel. A well-fitting dynamic model of yield curve dynamics must match not only the historical facts concerning the average shape of the yield curve and the variety of shapes assumed at different times, but also the dynamic *evolution* of those shapes.

For a parsimonious model to accord with all observed shapes and dynamic patterns is not easy, but let us consider some of the most important stylized facts and see whether and how DNS is capable of replicating them:

(1) *The average yield curve is increasing and concave.*

In our framework, the average yield curve is the yield curve corresponding to the average values of l_t, s_t, and c_t. It is certainly possible in principle that it may be increasing and concave, depending on the average values of l_t, s_t, and c_t.

---

[20] Gürkaynak et al. (2007) actually use a very close four-factor variant of Nelson-Siegel, which we introduce in the next chapter.

(2) *The yield curve takes a variety of shapes, including upward sloping, downward sloping ("inverted"), humped, and inverted humped.*

In our framework, the yield curve can assume all of those shapes. Whether and how often it does depends upon the values of, and variation in, l_t, s_t, and c_t.

(3) *Yield dynamics are highly persistent, and spread dynamics are much less persistent.*

In our framework, persistent yield dynamics correspond to strong persistence of l_t, as all yields load equally on l_t, which is certainly possible. In addition, if yield persistence is largely driven by common dependence on l_t, then the l_t effect should be eliminated by moving to spreads, which will then be less persistent.

Alternatively, spread dynamics that are less persistent could also be reflected in less persistence of s_t, as the yield curve slope is closely related to the long–short spread. This behavior is certainly possible in the DNS framework.

The key is to recognize that DNS distills a time series of yield curves into a three-variable time series of yield factors, so that different sorts of factor dynamics produce different sorts of yield curve dynamics.

Now consider DNS forecasts. In the DNS framework, forecasting the yield curve just amounts to forecasting a three-variable time series of factors. An obvious simple choice of model for the factors is a first-order vector autoregression. Beginning with the original paper of Diebold and Li (2006), however, many have noticed that an unrestricted vector autoregression is outperformed by a restricted version with diagonal coefficient matrix and innovation covariance matrix. Such "orthogonal state variables" are motivated by the common empirical finding that the DNS level, slope, and curvature factors are quite close (although of course not identical) to the first three yield principal components, which are orthogonal by construction. Recently some authors even work with theoretical models that force orthogonality, as in Lengwiler and Lenz (2010).

Figure 2.2 provides a good stylized summary of typical DNS forecast performance. For 1-, 6-, and 12-month forecast horizons and a variety of maturities, we show out-of-sample DNS root mean squared forecast error relative to that of a "no-change" (random walk) forecast. Several important results emerge.

First, the one-month DNS forecasts fare no better than no-change forecasts. This is unsurprising insofar as one month is quite a short horizon, at which the yield-factor mean reversion captured by DNS may have insufficient time to operate. To see this, consider, for example, one-*minute*-ahead yield curve forecasts, in which case "no change" is likely to be unbeatable!

Second, as the horizon lengthens somewhat to 6-month and 12-month, the relative performance of DNS improves dramatically. The intuition is the same: Although "no change" is a good approximation to the optimal forecast at the shortest horizons, it's a poor forecast at longer horizons, because it fails to capture the mean reversion in yield factors. Hence DNS fails to beat no change at the shortest horizons but beats it soundly at longer horizons. Empirically, it often happens that relative DNS performance is optimized at 6- to 12-month horizons.[21]

---

[21] At extremely long horizons the relative DNS performance again deteriorates, as both forecasts are poor—the no-change forecast is the current yield curve as always, and the DNS forecast is effectively the unconditional mean yield curve.

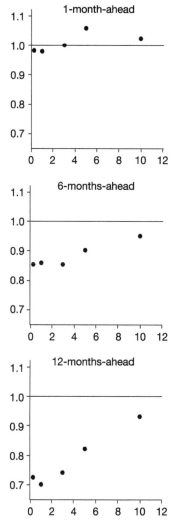

Figure 2.2. Out-of-Sample Forecasting Performance: DNS vs. Random Walk. For three forecast horizons and a variety of maturities, we show out-of-sample DNS root mean squared forecast error relative to that of a "no-change" forecast.

This may be particularly useful, as such horizons correspond to typical holding periods in many asset allocation strategies.

Third, the forecast accuracy gains delivered by DNS tend to come at short and medium maturities. We will have more to say about that in subsequent chapters when we introduce additional yield factors.

In closing, we would like to elaborate on the likely reason for DNS's forecasting success: DNS imposes a variety of restrictions, which of course degrade in-sample fit, but which may nevertheless be helpful for out-of-sample forecasting. The essence of our approach is intentionally to impose substantial a priori structure, motivated by simplicity, parsimony, and theory, in an explicit attempt to avoid data mining and hence enhance out-of-sample forecasts in the small samples encountered in practice. This includes our use of a tightly parametric model that places strict structure on factor loadings in accordance with simple theoretical desiderata for the discount function, our emphasis on simple univariate modeling of the factors based upon our theoretically derived interpretation of the model as one of approximately orthogonal level, slope, and curvature factors, and our emphasis on the simplest possible orthogonal AR(1) factor dynamics.

3

Arbitrage-Free Nelson-Siegel

Because bonds trade in deep and well-organized markets, the theoretical restrictions that eliminate opportunities for riskless arbitrage across maturities and over time hold powerful appeal, and they provide the foundation for a large finance literature on arbitrage-free models that started with Vasicek (1977) and Cox et al. (1985). Those models specify the risk-neutral evolution of the underlying yield curve factors as well as the dynamics of risk premia. Following Duffie and Kan (1996), the affine versions of those models are particularly popular, because yields are convenient affine functions of underlying latent factors with factor loadings that can be calculated from a simple system of differential equations.[1]

Unfortunately, the canonical affine arbitrage-free models often exhibit poor empirical time-series performance, especially when forecasting future yields, a point forcefully made by Duffee (2002). In addition, and crucially, the estimation of those models is known to be problematic, in large part because of the existence of numerous likelihood maxima that have essentially identical fit to the data but very different implications for economic behavior. These empirical problems appear to reflect a pervasive model overparameterization; as a solution,

---

[1] Piazzesi (2010) provides an insightful survey of affine arbitrage-free term structure models.

many researchers (e.g., Duffee (2002); Dai and Singleton (2002)) simply restrict to zero those parameters with small *t*-statistics in a first round of estimation. Joslin et al. (2010) put it well:

> Faced with such a large number of free parameters, standard practice has been to estimate a maximally flexible dynamic term structure model, set to zero many of the parameters . . . that are statistically insignificant at a conventional significance level, and then to analyze the constrained model. (p. 14)

The resulting more parsimonious structure is typically somewhat easier to estimate and has fewer troublesome likelihood maxima. However, the additional restrictions on model structure are not well motivated theoretically or statistically, and their arbitrary application and the computational burden of estimation effectively preclude robust model validation and thorough simulation studies of the finite-sample properties of the estimators.

In this chapter, we discuss a new class of affine arbitrage-free models that overcome the problems with empirical implementation of the canonical affine arbitrage-free model. This new class is based on DNS and retains its empirical tractability. Thus, from one perspective, we take the theoretically rigorous but empirically problematic affine arbitrage-free model and make it empirically tractable by incorporating DNS elements.

From an alternative perspective, we take the DNS model and make it theoretically more satisfactory. Let us elaborate. As we have emphasized, DNS is simple and stable to estimate, and it is quite flexible and fits both the cross section and time series of yields remarkably well. Theoretically, DNS imposes certain economically desirable properties, such as requiring the discount function to approach zero with maturity, and as we have shown, it corresponds to a modern three-factor model of time-varying level, slope, and curvature. However, despite its good empirical performance and a certain amount of theoretical appeal, DNS fails on an important theoretical dimension: It does not impose the restrictions necessary to eliminate opportunities for riskless arbitrage, as shown by Björk and Christensen (1999) and Filipović (1999, 2000).[2]

The lack of freedom from arbitrage motivated Diebold et al. (2005) and Christensen et al. (2011a) to introduce the class of arbitrage-free Nelson-Siegel (AFNS) yield curve models, which are affine arbitrage-free term structure models that nevertheless maintain the DNS factor-loading structure.

Diebold et al. (2005) considered a two-factor (level and slope) version of DNS to emphasize how the factor loadings used to represent the cross section of yields need to be consistent with the time-series properties of the state variables. They were silent, however, regarding the time-invariant "yield-adjustment term" required to make two-factor DNS fully arbitrage-free. Christensen et al. (2011a) considered the full three-factor DNS model and also explicitly characterized the yield-adjustment term, showing how DNS can be adjusted to fall within the Duffie-Kan class of arbitrage-free models. As we shall show, the approximation is almost exact. That is, DNS is almost arbitrage-free, as is. DNS requires only a time-invariant yield-adjustment term, which accounts for Jensen's inequality effects, to make it completely arbitrage-free.

---

[2] Recent work expanding on the Filipović-Bjork-Christensen insight includes Diebold et al. (2005). See also the additional references and discussion in Filipović (2009).

3.1   A Two-Factor Warm-Up

The two-factor Nelson-Siegel model studied in Diebold et al. (2005) specifies the yield on a τ-period bond as

$$y_t^{(\tau)} = a_\tau^{NS} + b_\tau^{NS} x_t, \tag{3.1}$$

where x_t is a two-dimensional vector of latent factors (or state variables) and the yield coefficients depend only on the time to maturity τ:

$$a_\tau^{NS} = 0, \tag{3.2}$$

$$b_\tau^{NS} = \left(1, \frac{1 - \exp(-k\tau)}{k\tau}\right)'. \tag{3.3}$$

The two coefficients in b_τ^{NS} give the loadings of yields on the two factors. The first loading is unity, so the first factor operates as a level shifter and affects yields of all maturities one-for-one. The second loading goes to one as $\tau \to 0$ and goes to zero as $\tau \to \infty$ (assuming $k > 0$), so the second factor mainly affects short maturities and, hence, the slope. Furthermore, as maturity τ goes to zero, the yield in equation (3.1) approaches the instantaneous short rate of interest, denoted r_t, and, since the second component of b_τ^{NS} goes to one, the short rate is just the sum of the two factors,

$$r_t = x_t^1 + x_t^2, \tag{3.4}$$

and is latent as well. Finally, as in Diebold and Li (2006), we augment the cross-sectional equation (3.1) with factor dynamics; specifically, both components of x_t are independent AR(1)'s:

$$x_t^i = \mu_i + \rho_i x_{t-1}^i + \upsilon_i \varepsilon_t^i, \tag{3.5}$$

with Gaussian errors ε_t^i, $i = 1, 2$. Therefore, the complete Nelson-Siegel dynamic representation, (3.1)–(3.5), has seven free parameters: k, $\mu_1, \rho_1, \upsilon_1, \mu_2, \rho_2$, and υ_2.

Consider now the two-factor affine no-arbitrage term-structure model. This model starts from the linear short-rate equation (3.4); however, rather than postulating a particular functional form for the factor loadings as above, the loadings are derived from the short-rate equation (3.4) and the factor dynamics (3.5) under the assumption of an absence of arbitrage opportunities. In particular, if there are risk-neutral investors, they are indifferent between buying a long bond that pays off $1 after τ periods and an investment that rolls over cash at the short rate during those τ periods and has an expected payoff of $1. Thus, risk-neutral investors would engage in arbitrage until the τ-period bond price equals the expected roll-over amount, so the yield on a τ-period bond will equal the expected average future short rate over the τ periods (plus a Jensen's inequality term). Risk-averse investors will need additional compensation for holding risky positions, but the same reasoning applies after correcting for risk premiums. Therefore, to make the Nelson-Siegel model internally consistent under the assumption of no-arbitrage, yields computed from expected future short rates using (3.4) with the factor dynamics (3.5) must be consistent with the cross-sectional specification in equations (3.1)–(3.3).

To enforce this no-arbitrage internal consistency, we switch to continuous time and fix the sampling frequency so that the interval $[t-1, t]$ covers, say, one month. The continuous-time AR(1) process corresponding to (3.5) is

$$dx_t^i = \kappa_i(\theta_i - x_t^i)dt + \sigma_i dB_t^i, \qquad (3.6)$$

where κ_i, θ_i, and σ_i are constants and B^i is a Brownian motion (which means that dB^i is normally distributed with mean zero and variance dt). (In continuous time, the Nelson-Siegel has seven parameters: k, $\kappa_1, \theta_1, \sigma_1, \kappa_2, \theta_2$, and σ_2.)

We first consider the model with risk-neutral investors, which consists of the linear short-rate equation (3.4) and the factor dynamics (3.6) and has six parameters: $\kappa_1, \theta_1, \sigma_1, \kappa_2, \theta_2$, and σ_2. Investors engage in arbitrage until the time-t price $P_t^{(\tau)}$ of the τ-bond is given by

$$P_t^{(\tau)} = E_t \left(\exp \left(- \int_t^{t+\tau} r_s ds \right) \right). \qquad (3.7)$$

This expectation can be computed by hand, since the short rate is the sum of two Gaussian AR(1)'s and is thus normally distributed. (Appendix A details these calculations.) The resulting τ-period yield is

$$y_t^{(\tau)} = - \frac{\log P_t^{(\tau)}}{\tau} = a_\tau^{NA} + b_\tau^{NA} x_t, \qquad (3.8)$$

with the no-arbitrage factor loadings given by

$$b_\tau^{NA} = \left(\frac{1 - \exp(-\kappa_1 \tau)}{\kappa_1 \tau}, \frac{1 - \exp(-\kappa_2 \tau)}{\kappa_2 \tau} \right)'. \qquad (3.9)$$

Equations (3.4), (3.6), (3.8), and (3.9) constitute a canonical affine term-structure specification with two Gaussian factors. Intuitively, in the risk-neutral world, where yields are based only on expected future short rates, the cross-sectional factor-loading coefficients b_τ^{NA} are restricted to be functions of the time-series parameters κ_1 and κ_2. The constant a_τ^{NA} absorbs any Jensen's inequality terms. In general, the Nelson-Siegel representation does not impose this dynamic consistency restriction because the loadings b_τ^{NS} are not related to the time-series parameters from the AR(1). However, the no-arbitrage restriction can be applied to the Nelson-Siegel model under two conditions. First, let κ_1 go to zero and set $\kappa_2 = k$, since, for these parameter values, $b_\tau^{NA} = b_\tau^{NS}$. Second, it will have to be the case that the constant a_τ^{NA}, which embeds the Jensen's inequality terms, is close to zero for reasonable parameter values, that is, $a_\tau^{NA} \approx a_\tau^{NS} = 0$. As a rule, macroeconomists often ignore Jensen's terms; however, with near–random walk components in the short-rate process as κ_1 goes to zero, the Jensen's terms may be large, especially for long maturities τ.[3]

Now consider the more general case of no-arbitrage with risk-averse investors. To accommodate departures from risk-neutrality, we parameterize the risk premiums used to adjust expectations. For example, suppose the pricing kernel solves

$$\frac{dm_t}{m_t} = -r_t dt - \lambda_t^1 dB_t^1 - \lambda_t^2 dB_t^2,$$

where

$$\lambda_t^i = \lambda_0^i + \lambda_1^i x_t^i$$

and λ_0^i, λ_1^i are constants. The variables λ_t^i are the prices of risk for each Brownian motion and are affine functions of the factors and so vary over time. The no-arbitrage factor loadings are[4]

$$b_\tau^{NA} = \left(\frac{1 - \exp\left(-\kappa_1^*\tau\right)}{\kappa_1^*\tau}, \frac{1 - \exp\left(-\kappa_2^*\tau\right)}{\kappa_2^*\tau} \right)', \quad (3.10)$$

where

$$\kappa_i^* = \kappa_i + \sigma_i \lambda_1^i.$$

This two-factor Gaussian model has 10 parameters: λ_0^1, λ_1^1, λ_0^2, λ_1^2, κ_1, θ_1, σ_1, κ_2, θ_2, and σ_2. Now it is possible to

---

[3] Indeed, results that we provide in section 3.3.2 show that, in the limit of zero mean reversion, $a_\tau^{NA} = \sigma_1^2 \cdot \tau^2/6$. As an example of the adjustment's magnitude for long maturities, consider an annualized volatility of 0.75 percentage point and a time to maturity of 30 years. Then we have $\sigma_1^2 \cdot \tau^2/6 = 0.0075^2 \cdot 30^2/6 = 0.0084375$, which is 0.844 percentage point, or 84.4 basis points.

[4] Again, see Appendix A.

pick the slope parameters, λ_1^i, so that the loadings, b_τ^{NA}, equal the Nelson-Siegel loadings, b_τ^{NS}. The values for λ_1^i that meet this condition are obtained by setting $\kappa_1^* = 0$ and $\kappa_2^* = k$, and these imply that

$$\lambda_1^1 = -\frac{\kappa_1}{\sigma_1} \quad \text{and} \quad \lambda_1^2 = \frac{k - \kappa_2}{\sigma_2}.$$

The constant terms in the market prices of risk are unrestricted, so we can set $\lambda_0^1 = \lambda_0^2 = 0$. Again, it will have to be case that the Jensen's inequality terms should be close to zero, so $a_\tau^{NA} \approx a_\tau^{NS} = 0$.

3.2   The Duffie-Kan Framework

Working in the standard continuous-time affine arbitrage-free environment of Duffie and Kan (1996), we make DNS arbitrage-free.[5] More precisely, we find the Duffie-Kan model with loadings closest to DNS. It turns out that there is a member of the Duffie-Kan class with loadings *exactly* equal to those of DNS.

We proceed in the affine diffusion environment of Duffie and Kan (1996), with a filtered probability space $(\Omega, \mathcal{F}, (\mathcal{F}_t), Q)$, where the filtration $(\mathcal{F}_t) = \{\mathcal{F}_t : t \geqslant 0\}$ satisfies the usual conditions.[6] The state variable X_t, a Markov process defined on a set $M \subset \mathbf{R}^n$, solves the stochastic differential equation (SDE)[7]

$$dX_t = K^Q(t) \left(\theta^Q(t) - X_t \right) dt + \Sigma(t) D(X_t, t) dW_t^Q, \tag{3.11}$$

where W^Q is a standard Brownian motion in $\mathbf{R}^n$, the information about which is contained in the filtration

---

[5] Krippner (2006) derives a special case of the AFNS model with constant risk premiums. See also Alfaro (2011).

[6] See, for example, Williams (1997).

[7] Note that (3.11) refers to the risk-neutral, or Q, dynamics.

$(\mathcal{F}_t)$. The drifts and dynamics $\theta^Q \colon [0,T] \to \mathbf{R}^n$ and $K^Q \colon [0,T] \to \mathbf{R}^{n \times n}$ are bounded, continuous functions.[8] Similarly, the volatility matrix $\Sigma \colon [0,T] \to \mathbf{R}^{n \times n}$ is a bounded, continuous function. The matrix $D \colon M \times [0,T] \to \mathbf{R}^{n \times n}$ is diagonal,

$$D(x_t, t)$$
$$= \begin{pmatrix} \sqrt{\gamma^1(t) + \delta^1(t) X_t} & \cdots & 0 \\ \vdots & \ddots & \vdots \\ 0 & \cdots & \sqrt{\gamma^n(t) + \delta^n(t) X_t} \end{pmatrix},$$

where $\delta^i(t)$ denotes the ith row of the matrix

$$\delta(t) = \begin{pmatrix} \delta_1^1(t) & \cdots & \delta_n^1(t) \\ \vdots & \ddots & \vdots \\ \delta_1^n(t) & \cdots & \delta_n^n(t) \end{pmatrix},$$

and $\gamma \colon [0,T] \to \mathbf{R}^n$ and $\delta \colon [0,T] \to \mathbf{R}^{n \times n}$ are bounded, continuous functions. Finally, the instantaneous risk-free rate is an affine function of the state variables,

$$r_t = \rho_0(t) + \rho_1(t)' X_t,$$

where $\rho_0 \colon [0,T] \to \mathbf{R}$ and $\rho_1 \colon [0,T] \to \mathbf{R}^n$ are bounded, continuous functions.

As shown by Duffie and Kan (1996), under the above assumptions zero-coupon bond prices are exponential-affine functions of the state variables,

$$P(t,T) = E_t^Q \left(\exp \left(- \int_t^T r_u du \right) \right)$$
$$= \exp \left(B(t,T)' X_t + C(t,T) \right),$$

---

[8] Stationarity of the state variables is ensured if the real components of all eigenvalues of $K^Q(t)$ are positive, as discussed, for example, in Ahn et al. (2002). However, stationarity is not necessary for the process to be well-defined.

where $B(t,T)$ and $C(t,T)$ are the solutions to the system of ordinary differential equations (ODEs)

$$\frac{dB(t,T)}{dt} = \rho_1 + (K^Q)'B(t,T)$$

$$- \frac{1}{2} \sum_{j=1}^{n} (\Sigma'B(t,T)B(t,T)'\Sigma)_{j,j}(\delta^j)',$$

$$\frac{dC(t,T)}{dt} = \rho_0 - B(t,T)'K^Q\theta^Q$$

$$- \frac{1}{2} \sum_{j=1}^{n} (\Sigma'B(t,T)B(t,T)'\Sigma)_{j,j}\gamma^j,$$

with $B(T,T) = 0$ and $C(T,T) = 0$.[9] The pricing functions imply that zero-coupon yields are

$$y(t,T) = -\frac{1}{T-t} \log P(t,T) = -\frac{B(t,T)'}{T-t}X_t - \frac{C(t,T)}{T-t}.$$

Hence, in particular, yields are also affine functions of the state variables.

3.3   Making DNS Arbitrage-Free

Our approach is to find the best approximation to DNS within the Duffie-Kan affine arbitrage-free class by finding the member(s) of the Duffie-Kan class with factor loadings closest to DNS. This is not the only way that one could proceed (i.e., it is not the only way to conceptualize "the best approximation to DNS within the Duffie-Kan affine arbitrage-free class"), but it is natural and intuitive, and it embodies our desire to find

---

[9] Note that for convenience we have adopted a notation that suppresses possible time dependence of the parameters.

a model that is simultaneously (1) parsimonious, accurate, and numerically tractable in the *P*-measure and (2) free from arbitrage. As regards (1), DNS is the obvious workhorse model, and as regards (2), Duffie-Kan is the obvious workhorse model. Our approach, which is introduced and developed in Christensen et al. (2011a), seeks the best of both worlds.

3.3.1 The Key Result

Given the pricing functions, for a three-factor affine model with $X_t = (X_t^1, X_t^2, X_t^3)$, the closest match to the Nelson-Siegel yield function is a yield function of the form

$$y(t, T) = X_t^1 + \frac{1 - e^{-\lambda(T-t)}}{\lambda(T-t)} X_t^2$$

$$+ \left(\frac{1 - e^{-\lambda(T-t)}}{\lambda(T-t)} - e^{-\lambda(T-t)} \right) X_t^3 - \frac{C(t, T)}{T-t},$$

with ODEs for the $B(t, T)$ functions with solutions

$$B^1(t, T) = -(T - t),$$

$$B^2(t, T) = -\frac{1 - e^{-\lambda(T-t)}}{\lambda},$$

$$B^3(t, T) = (T - t)e^{-\lambda(T-t)} - \frac{1 - e^{-\lambda(T-t)}}{\lambda}.$$

In this case the factor loadings exactly match DNS.[10] As described in the following proposition, there exists a member of the Duffie-Kan class that satisfies the above ODEs.

---

[10] Note that there is also an unavoidable "yield-adjustment term," $-C(t, T)/(T-t)$, which depends only on maturity, not on time. We will soon discuss this yield-adjustment term in detail.

Proposition (Proposition AFNS). *Suppose that the instantaneous risk-free rate is*

$$r_t = X_t^1 + X_t^2,$$

where the state variables $X_t = (X_t^1, X_t^2, X_t^3)$ *have risk-neutral* (Q) *dynamics:*

$$
\begin{pmatrix} dX_t^1 \\ dX_t^2 \\ dX_t^3 \end{pmatrix} = \begin{pmatrix} 0 & 0 & 0 \\ 0 & \lambda & -\lambda \\ 0 & 0 & \lambda \end{pmatrix} \left[\begin{pmatrix} \theta_1^Q \\ \theta_2^Q \\ \theta_3^Q \end{pmatrix} - \begin{pmatrix} X_t^1 \\ X_t^2 \\ X_t^3 \end{pmatrix} \right] dt
$$
$$
+ \begin{pmatrix} \sigma_{11} & \sigma_{12} & \sigma_{13} \\ \sigma_{21} & \sigma_{22} & \sigma_{23} \\ \sigma_{31} & \sigma_{32} & \sigma_{33} \end{pmatrix} \begin{pmatrix} dW_t^{1,Q} \\ dW_t^{2,Q} \\ dW_t^{3,Q} \end{pmatrix}, \quad \lambda > 0.
$$

$$(3.12)$$

Then zero-coupon bond prices are

$$
P(t,T) = E_t^Q \left(\exp \left(- \int_t^T r_u du \right) \right)
$$
$$
= \exp(B^1(t,T)X_t^1 + B^2(t,T)X_t^2
$$
$$
+ B^3(t,T)X_t^3 + C(t,T)),
$$

where $B^1(t,T)$, $B^2(t,T)$, $B^3(t,T)$, *and* $C(t,T)$ *are governed by the ODEs:*

$$
\begin{pmatrix} \dfrac{dB^1(t,T)}{dt} \\[2mm] \dfrac{dB^2(t,T)}{dt} \\[2mm] \dfrac{dB^3(t,T)}{dt} \end{pmatrix} = \begin{pmatrix} 1 \\ 1 \\ 0 \end{pmatrix} + \begin{pmatrix} 0 & 0 & 0 \\ 0 & \lambda & 0 \\ 0 & -\lambda & \lambda \end{pmatrix} \begin{pmatrix} B^1(t,T) \\ B^2(t,T) \\ B^3(t,T) \end{pmatrix},
$$

$$\frac{dC(t,T)}{dt} = -B(t,T)'^Q\theta^Q$$

$$-\frac{1}{2}\sum_{j=1}^{3}(\Sigma'B(t,T)B(t,T)'\Sigma)_{j,j}$$

(with boundary conditions $B^1(T,T) = B^2(T,T) = B^3(T,T) = C(T,T) = 0$), with solution

$$B^1(t,T) = -(T-t)$$

$$B^2(t,T) = -\frac{1-e^{-\lambda(T-t)}}{\lambda},$$

$$B^3(t,T) = (T-t)e^{-\lambda(T-t)} - \frac{1-e^{-\lambda(T-t)}}{\lambda},$$

$$C(t,T) = (K^Q\theta^Q)_2\int_t^T B^2(s,T)ds$$

$$+ (K^Q\theta^Q)_3\int_t^T B^3(s,T)ds$$

$$+ \frac{1}{2}\sum_{j=1}^{3}\int_t^T \left(\Sigma'B(s,T)B(s,T)'\Sigma\right)_{j,j}ds.$$

Hence zero-coupon bond yields are

$$y(t,T) = X_t^1 + \frac{1-e^{-\lambda(T-t)}}{\lambda(T-t)}X_t^2$$

$$+ \left[\frac{1-e^{-\lambda(T-t)}}{\lambda(T-t)} - e^{-\lambda(T-t)}\right]X_t^3 - \frac{C(t,T)}{T-t}.$$

Proof. The system of ODEs for $B(t,T)$ is

$$\frac{dB(t,T)}{dt} = \rho_1 + (K^Q)'B(t,T), \quad B(T,T) = 0.$$

Because

$$\frac{d}{dt}\left(e^{(K^Q)'(T-t)}B(t,T)\right) = e^{(K^Q)'(T-t)}\frac{dB(t,T)}{dt}$$
$$- (K^Q)'e^{(K^Q)'(T-t)}B(t,T),$$

it follows from the system of ODEs that

$$\int_t^T \frac{d}{ds}\left[e^{(K^Q)'(T-s)}B(s,T)\right]ds = \int_t^T e^{(K^Q)'(T-s)}\rho_1 ds,$$

or, equivalently, using the boundary conditions,

$$B(t,T) = -e^{-(K^Q)'(T-t)}\int_t^T e^{(K^Q)'(T-s)}\rho_1 ds.$$

Now impose the following structure on $(K^Q)'$ and ρ_1:

$$(K^Q)' = \begin{pmatrix} 0 & 0 & 0 \\ 0 & \lambda & 0 \\ 0 & -\lambda & \lambda \end{pmatrix} \quad \text{and} \quad \rho_1 = \begin{pmatrix} 1 \\ 1 \\ 0 \end{pmatrix}.$$

It is then easy to show that

$$e^{(K^Q)'(T-t)} = \begin{pmatrix} 1 & 0 & 0 \\ 0 & e^{\lambda(T-t)} & 0 \\ 0 & -\lambda(T-t)e^{\lambda(T-t)} & e^{\lambda(T-t)} \end{pmatrix}$$

and

$$e^{-(K^Q)'(T-t)} = \begin{pmatrix} 1 & 0 & 0 \\ 0 & e^{-\lambda(T-t)} & 0 \\ 0 & \lambda(T-t)e^{-\lambda(T-t)} & e^{-\lambda(T-t)} \end{pmatrix}.$$

Inserting this in the ODE, we obtain

$$B(t,T) = -\begin{pmatrix} 1 & 0 & 0 \\ 0 & e^{-\lambda(T-t)} & 0 \\ 0 & \lambda(T-t)e^{-\lambda(T-t)} & e^{-\lambda(T-t)} \end{pmatrix}$$

$$\times \int_t^T \begin{pmatrix} 1 \\ e^{\lambda(T-s)} \\ -\lambda(T-s)e^{\lambda(T-s)} \end{pmatrix} ds.$$

Now, because

$$\int_t^T ds = T - t$$

and

$$\int_t^T e^{\lambda(T-s)} ds = \left[\frac{-1}{\lambda} e^{\lambda(T-s)} \right]_t^T = -\frac{1 - e^{\lambda(T-t)}}{\lambda}$$

and

$$\int_t^T -\lambda(T-s)e^{\lambda(T-s)} ds$$

$$= \frac{1}{\lambda} \int_{\lambda(T-t)}^0 xe^x dx$$

$$= \frac{1}{\lambda} [xe^x]_{\lambda(T-t)}^0 - \frac{1}{\lambda} \int_{\lambda(T-t)}^0 e^x dx$$

$$= -(T-t)e^{\lambda(T-t)} - \frac{1 - e^{\lambda(T-t)}}{\lambda},$$

the system of ODEs can be reduced to $B(t,T) = A \times B$, where

$$A = -\begin{pmatrix} 1 & 0 & 0 \\ 0 & e^{-\lambda(T-t)} & 0 \\ 0 & \lambda(T-t)e^{-\lambda(T-t)} & e^{-\lambda(T-t)} \end{pmatrix}$$

and

$$B = \begin{pmatrix} T - t \\ -\dfrac{1 - e^{\lambda(T-t)}}{\lambda} \\ -(T-t)e^{\lambda(T-t)} - \dfrac{1 - e^{\lambda(T-t)}}{\lambda} \end{pmatrix}.$$

Hence

$$B(t,T) = \begin{pmatrix} -(T-t) \\ -\dfrac{1 - e^{-\lambda(T-t)}}{\lambda} \\ (T-t)e^{-\lambda(T-t)} - \dfrac{1 - e^{-\lambda(T-t)}}{\lambda} \end{pmatrix},$$

which matches the claim in Proposition AFNS.   □

The AFNS model is related to the work of Trolle and Schwartz (2009), who show that the dynamics of the forward rate curve in a general m-dimensional Heath et al. (1992) model can always be represented by a finite-dimensional Markov process with time-homogeneous volatility structure if each volatility function is given by

$$\sigma_i(t,T) = p_{n,i}(T-t)e^{-\gamma_i(T-t)}, \quad i = 1, \ldots, m, \quad (3.13)$$

where $p_{n,i}(\tau)$ is an n-order polynomial in τ. Because the forward rates in the DNS model satisfy this requirement, there exists such an arbitrage-free three-dimensional Heath-Jarrow-Morton model.

Proposition AFNS has several interesting implications. First, the three state variables are Gaussian Ornstein-Uhlenbeck processes with constant volatility matrix Σ.[11] The instantaneous interest rate is the sum of level and

---

[11] Proposition AFNS can be extended to include jumps in the state variables. As long as the jump arrival intensity is state-independent, the Nelson-Siegel factor-loading structure in the yield

slope factors (X_t^1 and X_t^2), while the sole role of the curvature factor (X_t^3) is as a stochastic time-varying mean for the slope factor under the Q-measure.

Second, Proposition AFNS provides insight into the nature of the parameter λ. Although a few authors (e.g., Koopman et al., 2010a) have considered time-varying λ, Proposition AFNS suggests that it should be constant. In the AFNS model, λ is the mean-reversion rate of the curvature and slope factors as well as the scale by which a deviation of the curvature factor from its mean affects the mean of the slope factor.

Third, and crucially, although the proposition clearly imposes significant structure (i.e., restrictions) on AFNS dynamics under the Q-measure, it places *no* structure on AFNS dynamics under the P-measure. In particular, the AFNS yield-adjustment term $-C(t,T)/(T - t)$, which is the key wedge between AFNS and DNS under the P-measure, depends only on maturity, not on time. We now provide a precise characterization of the yield-adjustment term.

3.3.2   The Yield-Adjustment Term

Following Christensen et al. (2011a), we identify the AFNS models by fixing the mean levels of the state variables under the Q-measure at 0, that is, $\theta^Q = 0$. This implies that the yield-adjustment term is of the form

$$\frac{C(t,T)}{T-t} = \frac{1}{2}\frac{1}{T-t}\sum_{j=1}^{3}\int_{t}^{T}\left(\Sigma' B(s,T)B(s,T)'\Sigma\right)_{j,j}ds.$$

In the following proposition we provide a precise analytic characterization.

---

function is maintained because only $C(t,T)$ is affected by the inclusion of such jumps. See Duffie et al. (2000) for the needed modification of the ODEs for $C(t,T)$ in this case.

Proposition (Proposition AFNS-adj). *The AFNS yield-adjustment term is*

$$\frac{C(t,T)}{T-t}$$

$$= \bar{A}\left(\frac{(T-t)^2}{6}\right)$$

$$+ \bar{B}\left(\frac{1}{2\lambda^2} - \frac{1}{\lambda^3}\frac{1-e^{-\lambda(T-t)}}{T-t} + \frac{1}{4\lambda^3}\frac{1-e^{-2\lambda(T-t)}}{T-t}\right)$$

$$+ \bar{C}\left(\frac{1}{2\lambda^2} + \frac{1}{\lambda^2}e^{-\lambda(T-t)} - \frac{1}{4\lambda}(T-t)e^{-2\lambda(T-t)}\right.$$

$$- \frac{3}{4\lambda^2}e^{-2\lambda(T-t)} - \frac{2}{\lambda^3}\frac{1-e^{-\lambda(T-t)}}{T-t}$$

$$\left. + \frac{5}{8\lambda^3}\frac{1-e^{-2\lambda(T-t)}}{T-t}\right)$$

$$+ \bar{D}\left(\frac{1}{2\lambda}(T-t) + \frac{1}{\lambda^2}e^{-\lambda(T-t)} - \frac{1}{\lambda^3}\frac{1-e^{-\lambda(T-t)}}{T-t}\right)$$

$$+ \bar{E}\left(\frac{3}{\lambda^2}e^{-\lambda(T-t)} + \frac{1}{2\lambda}(T-t)\right.$$

$$\left. + \frac{1}{\lambda}(T-t)e^{-\lambda(T-t)} - \frac{3}{\lambda^3}\frac{1-e^{-\lambda(T-t)}}{T-t}\right)$$

$$+ \bar{F}\left(\frac{1}{\lambda^2} + \frac{1}{\lambda^2}e^{-\lambda(T-t)} - \frac{1}{2\lambda^2}e^{-2\lambda(T-t)}\right.$$

$$\left. - \frac{3}{\lambda^3}\frac{1-e^{-\lambda(T-t)}}{T-t} + \frac{3}{4\lambda^3}\frac{1-e^{-2\lambda(T-t)}}{T-t}\right),$$

where

$$\bar{A} = \sigma_{11}^2 + \sigma_{12}^2 + \sigma_{13}^2,$$
$$\bar{B} = \sigma_{21}^2 + \sigma_{22}^2 + \sigma_{23}^2,$$
$$\bar{C} = \sigma_{31}^2 + \sigma_{32}^2 + \sigma_{33}^2,$$

$$\bar{D} = \sigma_{11}\sigma_{21} + \sigma_{12}\sigma_{22} + \sigma_{13}\sigma_{23},$$
$$\bar{E} = \sigma_{11}\sigma_{31} + \sigma_{12}\sigma_{32} + \sigma_{13}\sigma_{33},$$
$$\bar{F} = \sigma_{21}\sigma_{31} + \sigma_{22}\sigma_{32} + \sigma_{23}\sigma_{33},$$

and

$$\Sigma = \begin{pmatrix} \sigma_{11} & \sigma_{12} & \sigma_{13} \\ \sigma_{21} & \sigma_{22} & \sigma_{23} \\ \sigma_{31} & \sigma_{32} & \sigma_{33} \end{pmatrix}.$$

Proof. In the AFNS model the yield-adjustment term is in general

$$\frac{C(t,T)}{T-t} = \frac{1}{2}\frac{1}{T-t}\int_t^T \sum_{j=1}^3 \left(\Sigma' B(s,T)B(s,T)'\Sigma\right)_{j,j} ds$$

$$= \frac{\bar{A}}{2}\frac{1}{T-t}\int_t^T B^1(s,T)^2 ds$$

$$+ \frac{\bar{B}}{2}\frac{1}{T-t}\int_t^T B^2(s,T)^2 ds$$

$$+ \frac{\bar{C}}{2}\frac{1}{T-t}\int_t^T B^3(s,T)^2 ds$$

$$+ \bar{D}\frac{1}{T-t}\int_t^T B^1(s,T)B^2(s,T) ds$$

$$+ \bar{E}\frac{1}{T-t}\int_t^T B^1(s,T)B^3(s,T) ds$$

$$+ \bar{F}\frac{1}{T-t}\int_t^T B^2(s,T)B^3(s,T) ds,$$

where

$$\bar{A} = \sigma_{11}^2 + \sigma_{12}^2 + \sigma_{13}^2,$$
$$\bar{B} = \sigma_{21}^2 + \sigma_{22}^2 + \sigma_{23}^2,$$
$$\bar{C} = \sigma_{31}^2 + \sigma_{32}^2 + \sigma_{33}^2,$$

$$\bar{D} = \sigma_{11}\sigma_{21} + \sigma_{12}\sigma_{22} + \sigma_{13}\sigma_{23},$$

$$\bar{E} = \sigma_{11}\sigma_{31} + \sigma_{12}\sigma_{32} + \sigma_{13}\sigma_{33},$$

$$\bar{F} = \sigma_{21}\sigma_{31} + \sigma_{22}\sigma_{32} + \sigma_{23}\sigma_{33}.$$

To derive the analytical formula for $C(t,T)/(T-t)$, six integrals need to be solved. The first is

$$I_1 = \frac{\bar{A}}{2}\frac{1}{T-t}\int_t^T B^1(s,T)^2 ds$$

$$= \frac{\bar{A}}{2}\frac{1}{T-t}\int_t^T (T-s)^2 ds = \frac{\bar{A}}{6}(T-t)^2.$$

The second is

$$I_2 = \frac{\bar{B}}{2}\frac{1}{T-t}\int_t^T B^2(s,T)ds$$

$$= \frac{\bar{B}}{2}\frac{1}{T-t}\int_t^T \left[-\frac{1-e^{-\lambda(T-s)}}{\lambda}\right]^2 ds$$

$$= \bar{B}\left[\frac{1}{2\lambda^2} - \frac{1}{\lambda^3}\frac{1-e^{-\lambda(T-t)}}{T-t} + \frac{1}{4\lambda^3}\frac{1-e^{-2\lambda(T-t)}}{T-t}\right].$$

The third is

$$I_3 = \frac{\bar{C}}{2}\frac{1}{T-t}\int_t^T B^3(s,T)ds$$

$$= \frac{\bar{C}}{2}\frac{1}{T-t}\int_t^T \left\{(T-s)e^{-\lambda(T-s)} - \frac{1-e^{-\lambda(T-s)}}{\lambda}\right\}^2 ds$$

$$= \bar{C}\left[\frac{1}{2\lambda^2} + \frac{1}{\lambda^2}e^{-\lambda(T-t)}\right.$$

$$- \frac{1}{4\lambda}(T-t)e^{-2\lambda(T-t)} - \frac{3}{4\lambda^2}e^{-2\lambda(T-t)}$$

$$\left. - \frac{2}{\lambda^3}\frac{1-e^{-\lambda(T-t)}}{T-t} + \frac{5}{8\lambda^3}\frac{1-e^{-2\lambda(T-t)}}{T-t}\right].$$

The fourth is

$$I_4 = \frac{\bar{D}}{T-t} \int_t^T B^1(s,T)B^2(s,T)ds$$

$$= \frac{\bar{D}}{T-t} \int_t^T [-(T-s)] \left[-\frac{1-e^{-\lambda(T-s)}}{\lambda} \right] ds$$

$$= \bar{D} \left[\frac{1}{2\lambda}(T-t) + \frac{1}{\lambda^2}e^{-\lambda(T-t)} - \frac{1}{\lambda^3} \frac{1-e^{-\lambda(T-t)}}{T-t} \right].$$

The fifth is

$$I_5 = \bar{E}\frac{1}{T-t} \int_t^T B^1(s,T)B^3(s,T)ds$$

$$= \bar{E}\frac{1}{T-t} \int_t^T [-(T-s)]$$

$$\times \left[(T-s)e^{-\lambda(T-s)} - \frac{1-e^{-\lambda(T-s)}}{\lambda} \right] ds$$

$$= \bar{E} \left[\frac{3}{\lambda^2}e^{-\lambda(T-t)} + \frac{1}{2\lambda}(T-t) \right.$$

$$\left. + \frac{1}{\lambda}(T-t)e^{-\lambda(T-t)} - \frac{3}{\lambda^3} \frac{1-e^{-\lambda(T-t)}}{T-t} \right].$$

The sixth is

$$I_6 = \bar{F}\frac{1}{T-t} \int_t^T B^2(s,T)B^3(s,T)ds$$

$$= \bar{F}\frac{1}{T-t} \int_t^T \left[-\frac{1-e^{-\lambda(T-s)}}{\lambda} \right]$$

$$\times \left[(T-s)e^{-\lambda(T-s)} - \frac{1-e^{-\lambda(T-s)}}{\lambda} \right] ds$$

$$= \bar{F} \left[\frac{1}{\lambda^2} + \frac{1}{\lambda^2}e^{-\lambda(T-t)} - \frac{1}{2\lambda^2}e^{-2\lambda(T-t)} \right.$$

$$\left. - \frac{3}{\lambda^3} \frac{1-e^{-\lambda(T-t)}}{T-t} + \frac{3}{4\lambda^3} \frac{1-e^{-2\lambda(T-t)}}{T-t} \right].$$

Combining the six integrals yields the claimed result. $\square$

Because Proposition AFNS-adj produces an analytical formula for bond yields, it greatly facilitates the empirical implementation of arbitrage-free models. It also makes clear that the nine underlying volatility parameters are not separately identified; only the six terms $\bar{A}$, $\bar{B}$, $\bar{C}$, $\bar{D}$, $\bar{E}$, and $\bar{F}$ can be identified. Hence the maximally flexible AFNS specification that can be identified has triangular volatility matrix

$$\Sigma = \begin{pmatrix} \sigma_{11} & 0 & 0 \\ \sigma_{21} & \sigma_{22} & 0 \\ \sigma_{31} & \sigma_{32} & \sigma_{33} \end{pmatrix}.$$

We have written the matrix as lower-triangular, but the choice of upper- or lower-triangular is inconsequential.

We close this section with a bit more discussion of the AFNS/DNS relationship. AFNS blends two important and successful approaches to yield curve modeling: the DNS empirically based one and the no-arbitrage theoretically based one. Yield curve models in both traditions are impressive successes, albeit for very different reasons. Ironically, both approaches are equally impressive failures, and for the same reasons, swapped. That is, models in the DNS tradition fit and forecast well, but they lack theoretical rigor insofar as they may admit arbitrage possibilities, while models in the arbitrage-free tradition are theoretically rigorous insofar as they enforce absence of arbitrage, but they may fit and forecast poorly. AFNS bridges the divide with a DNS-inspired model that enforces absence of arbitrage. Approached from the arbitrage-free side, AFNS maintains the arbitrage-free theoretical restrictions of the canonical affine models but can be easily estimated, because the dynamic Nelson-Siegel structure helps identify the latent yield curve factors and delivers analytical solutions for zero-coupon bond prices. Approached from the DNS side, AFNS maintains the simplicity and empirical tractability of the popular DNS model, while simultaneously enforcing the theoretically desirable property of absence of riskless arbitrage.

3.3.3 On the Bjork-Christensen-Filipović Critique and the Yield-Adjustment Term

Recall the Bjork-Christensen-Filipović critique discussed in the introduction to this chapter. The Nelson-Siegel curve corresponds to an economy with yields evolving deterministically according to a second-order differential equation. Fitting the Nelson-Siegel curve to observed yields on a regular basis, however, reveals that the three Nelson-Siegel factors vary dynamically and stochastically. The question then becomes: Are the Nelson-Siegel bond prices dynamically consistent in that they do not admit arbitrage opportunities? Or technically: Are discounted bond prices semimartingales? Björk and Christensen (1999) and Filipović (1999) effectively ask this question, phrasing it more completely as: Does there exist a diffusion process for three factors that delivers the Nelson-Siegel yield function while simultaneously ensuring absence of arbitrage? They show that the answer is no.

At this point, then, having made DNS arbitrage-free (Proposition AFNS) and completely characterized the associated yield-adjustment term (Proposition AFNS-adj), it is worth stepping back to think about the big picture. In particular, what is the intuition for how and why AFNS "works," and how does it escape the Bjork-Christensen-Filipović critique?

The answer is very simple. The Nelson-Siegel model admits arbitrage because it has a deterministic foundation and therefore fails to account for the convexity arising from Jensen's inequality effects when yield factors are stochastic. Equivalently but put quite differently, the Nelson-Siegel model cannot enforce no-arbitrage because the parameters that determine the dynamic evolution of the yield curve factors (i.e., the parameters of the state equation) are not linked to the parameters that determine the shape and location of the yield curve (i.e., the parameters of the measurement equation). AFNS supplies the missing piece via the yield-adjustment term, which links the transition and measurement equations in a way that ensures that discounted bond prices are semimartingales and therefore arbitrage-free.[12]

It is easy to (mis-)read Björk and Christensen (1999) and Filipović (1999) and conclude erroneously that DNS cannot be made arbitrage-free. In reality those papers show only that DNS is not arbitrage-free, not that DNS can't be made arbitrage-free. Hence our Propositions AFNS and AFNS-adj are in no way inconsistent with Björk and Christensen (1999) and Filipović (1999). Moreover, Propositions AFNS and AFNS-adj reveal that DNS is "almost" arbitrage-free; one only need add a simple time-invariant adjustment to take it all the way there.

3.4   Workhorse Models

In general, the DNS and AFNS models are silent about the P-dynamics, so there are an infinite number of possible specifications that could be used. Here we introduce two important versions of the DNS and AFNS models that have featured prominently in the literature. In

---

[12] Steeley (2011) develops a shape-based decomposition of the AFNS yield-adjustment term and shows that it is dominated by a quadratic function of maturity directly linked to Jensen's inequality effects.

subsequent sections, we use them to help organize our thoughts about the restrictions implicit in AFNS and about empirical AFNS results.

In the *independent-factor DNS model*, the three state variables are independent first-order autoregressions, as in Diebold and Li (2006). The state transition equation is

$$
\begin{pmatrix} L_t - \mu_L \\ S_t - \mu_S \\ C_t - \mu_C \end{pmatrix}
$$

$$
= \begin{pmatrix} a_{11} & 0 & 0 \\ 0 & a_{22} & 0 \\ 0 & 0 & a_{33} \end{pmatrix} \begin{pmatrix} L_{t-1} - \mu_L \\ S_{t-1} - \mu_S \\ C_{t-1} - \mu_C \end{pmatrix} + \begin{pmatrix} \eta_t(L) \\ \eta_t(S) \\ \eta_t(C) \end{pmatrix},
$$

where the stochastic shocks $\eta_t(L)$, $\eta_t(S)$, and $\eta_t(C)$ have covariance matrix

$$
Q = \begin{pmatrix} q_{11}^2 & 0 & 0 \\ 0 & q_{22}^2 & 0 \\ 0 & 0 & q_{33}^2 \end{pmatrix}.
$$

In the *correlated-factor DNS model*, the state variables follow a first-order vector autoregression, as in Diebold et al. (2006b). The transition equation is

$$
\begin{pmatrix} L_t - \mu_L \\ S_t - \mu_S \\ C_t - \mu_C \end{pmatrix}
$$

$$
= \begin{pmatrix} a_{11} & a_{12} & a_{13} \\ a_{21} & a_{22} & a_{23} \\ a_{31} & a_{32} & a_{33} \end{pmatrix} \begin{pmatrix} L_{t-1} - \mu_L \\ S_{t-1} - \mu_S \\ C_{t-1} - \mu_C \end{pmatrix} + \begin{pmatrix} \eta_t(L) \\ \eta_t(S) \\ \eta_t(C) \end{pmatrix},
$$

where the stochastic shocks $\eta_t(L)$, $\eta_t(S)$, and $\eta_t(C)$ have covariance matrix $Q = qq'$, where

$$q = \begin{pmatrix} q_{11} & 0 & 0 \\ q_{21} & q_{22} & 0 \\ q_{31} & q_{32} & q_{33} \end{pmatrix}.$$

In both the independent-factor and correlated-factor DNS models, the measurement equation is

$$\begin{pmatrix} y_t(\tau_1) \\ y_t(\tau_2) \\ \vdots \\ y_t(\tau_N) \end{pmatrix}$$

$$= \begin{pmatrix} 1 & \dfrac{1 - e^{-\lambda\tau_1}}{\lambda\tau_1} & \dfrac{1 - e^{-\lambda\tau_1}}{\lambda\tau_1} - e^{-\lambda\tau_1} \\ 1 & \dfrac{1 - e^{-\lambda\tau_2}}{\lambda\tau_2} & \dfrac{1 - e^{-\lambda\tau_2}}{\lambda\tau_2} - e^{-\lambda\tau_2} \\ \vdots & \vdots & \vdots \\ 1 & \dfrac{1 - e^{-\lambda\tau_N}}{\lambda\tau_N} & \dfrac{1 - e^{-\lambda\tau_N}}{\lambda\tau_N} - e^{-\lambda\tau_N} \end{pmatrix} \begin{pmatrix} L_t \\ S_t \\ C_t \end{pmatrix}$$

$$+ \begin{pmatrix} \varepsilon_t(\tau_1) \\ \varepsilon_t(\tau_2) \\ \vdots \\ \varepsilon_t(\tau_N) \end{pmatrix},$$

$$(3.14)$$

where the measurement errors $\varepsilon_t(\tau_i)$ are i.i.d. white noise.

Following Christensen et al. (2011), we formulate the corresponding AFNS models in continuous time. The relationship between the real-world dynamics under the P-measure and the risk-neutral dynamics under the

Q-measure is

$$dW_t^Q = dW_t^P + \Gamma_t dt,$$

where Γ_t is the risk premium. We limit our focus to essentially affine risk premium specifications (see Duffee, 2002), in which Γ_t is affine in the state variables X_t,

$$\Gamma_t = \begin{pmatrix} \alpha\gamma_1^0 \\ \gamma_2^0 \\ \gamma_3^0 \end{pmatrix} + \begin{pmatrix} \gamma_{11}^1 & \gamma_{12}^1 & \gamma_{13}^1 \\ \gamma_{21}^1 & \gamma_{22}^1 & \gamma_{23}^1 \\ \gamma_{31}^1 & \gamma_{32}^1 & \gamma_{33}^1 \end{pmatrix} \begin{pmatrix} X_t^1 \\ X_t^2 \\ X_t^3 \end{pmatrix}.$$

The essentially affine risk premium specification preserves affine dynamics under the P-measure; that is, the P-measure dynamics,

$$dX_t = K^P[\theta^P - X_t]dt + \Sigma dW_t^P, \qquad (3.15)$$

remain affine. Put differently, due to the flexible specification of Γ_t we are free to choose any mean vector θ^P and mean-reversion matrix K^P under the P-measure and still preserve the required Q-dynamic structure described in Proposition AFNS. Hence we focus on the two AFNS models that correspond to the independent-factor and correlated-factor DNS models above.

In the *independent-factor AFNS model*, the three state variables are independent under the P-measure,

$$\begin{pmatrix} dX_t^1 \\ dX_t^2 \\ dX_t^3 \end{pmatrix} = \begin{pmatrix} \kappa_{11}^P & 0 & 0 \\ 0 & \kappa_{22}^P & 0 \\ 0 & 0 & \kappa_{33}^P \end{pmatrix} \left[\begin{pmatrix} \theta_1^P \\ \theta_2^P \\ \theta_3^P \end{pmatrix} - \begin{pmatrix} X_t^1 \\ X_t^2 \\ X_t^3 \end{pmatrix} \right] dt$$
$$+ \begin{pmatrix} \sigma_1 & 0 & 0 \\ 0 & \sigma_2 & 0 \\ 0 & 0 & \sigma_3 \end{pmatrix} \begin{pmatrix} dW_t^{1,P} \\ dW_t^{2,P} \\ dW_t^{3,P} \end{pmatrix}.$$

In the *correlated-factor AFNS model*, the three state variables may interact dynamically and/or their shocks may be correlated,

$$
\begin{pmatrix} dX_t^1 \\ dX_t^2 \\ dX_t^3 \end{pmatrix} = \begin{pmatrix} \kappa_{11}^P & \kappa_{12}^P & \kappa_{13}^P \\ \kappa_{21}^P & \kappa_{22}^P & \kappa_{23}^P \\ \kappa_{31}^P & \kappa_{32}^P & \kappa_{33}^P \end{pmatrix} \left[\begin{pmatrix} \theta_1^P \\ \theta_2^P \\ \theta_3^P \end{pmatrix} - \begin{pmatrix} X_t^1 \\ X_t^2 \\ X_t^3 \end{pmatrix} \right] dt
$$
$$
+ \begin{pmatrix} \sigma_{11} & 0 & 0 \\ \sigma_{21} & \sigma_{22} & 0 \\ \sigma_{31} & \sigma_{32} & \sigma_{33} \end{pmatrix} \begin{pmatrix} dW_t^{1,P} \\ dW_t^{2,P} \\ dW_t^{3,P} \end{pmatrix}.
$$

Correlated-factor AFNS is the most flexible AFNS model with all parameters identified. In both the independent-factor and correlated-factor AFNS models, the measurement equation is

$$
\begin{pmatrix} y_t(\tau_1) \\ y_t(\tau_2) \\ \vdots \\ y_t(\tau_N) \end{pmatrix} = \begin{pmatrix} 1 & \dfrac{1-e^{-\lambda\tau_1}}{\lambda\tau_1} & \dfrac{1-e^{-\lambda\tau_1}}{\lambda\tau_1} - e^{-\lambda\tau_1} \\ 1 & \dfrac{1-e^{-\lambda\tau_2}}{\lambda\tau_2} & \dfrac{1-e^{-\lambda\tau_2}}{\lambda\tau_2} - e^{-\lambda\tau_2} \\ \vdots & \vdots & \vdots \\ 1 & \dfrac{1-e^{-\lambda\tau_N}}{\lambda\tau_N} & \dfrac{1-e^{-\lambda\tau_N}}{\lambda\tau_N} - e^{-\lambda\tau_N} \end{pmatrix} \begin{pmatrix} X_t^1 \\ X_t^2 \\ X_t^3 \end{pmatrix}
$$
$$
- \begin{pmatrix} \dfrac{C(\tau_1)}{\tau^1} \\ \dfrac{C(\tau_2)}{\tau^2} \\ \vdots \\ \dfrac{C(\tau_N)}{\tau^N} \end{pmatrix} + \begin{pmatrix} \varepsilon_t(\tau_1) \\ \varepsilon_t(\tau_2) \\ \vdots \\ \varepsilon_t(\tau_N) \end{pmatrix},
$$

where the measurement errors $\varepsilon_t(\tau_i)$ are i.i.d. noise.

3.5 AFNS Restrictions on $A_0(3)$

The AFNS model is a member of the Dai and Singleton (2000) canonical $A_0(3)$ class of affine arbitrage-free models, which have three state variables, none of which drive square-root variance processes.[13]

The fact that AFNS is $A_0(3)$ as opposed to $A_m(N)$ for some $N > 3$ and/or $m > 0$ makes clear that it involves restrictions. Moreover, and interestingly, AFNS involves restrictions even relative to the $A_0(3)$ class. Here we explore and characterize the restrictions that AFNS places on the maximally flexible canonical $A_0(3)$ affine arbitrage-free model.

Denoting the state variables by Y_t, the canonical $A_0(3)$ model is

$$r_t = \delta_0^n + (\delta_1^n)' Y_t,$$
$$dY_t = K_n^P[\theta_n^P - Y_t]dt + \Sigma_n dW_t^P,$$
$$dY_t = K_n^Q[\theta_n^Q - Y_t]dt + \Sigma_n dW_t^Q,$$

with $\delta_0^n \in \mathbf{R}$, $\delta_1^n, \theta_n^P, \theta_n^Q \in \mathbf{R}^3$, and $K_n^P, K_n^Q, \Sigma_n \in \mathbf{R}^{3\times3}$.[14] If the essentially affine risk premium specification $\Gamma_t = \gamma_n^0 + \gamma_n^1 Y_t$ is imposed on the model, the drift terms under the P-measure (K_n^P, θ_n^P) can be chosen independently of the drift terms under the Q-measure (K_n^Q, θ_n^Q).

bECAUSE the latent state variables may rotate without changing the probability distribution of bond yields,

---

[13] In general $A_m(N)$ refers to a representation with N state variables driving m square-root variance processes. For an insightful exposition see Singleton (2006), Chapter 12.

[14] Note that Y_t denotes the state variables of the canonical representation, which are different from the X_t state variables in the AFNS models, and that subscripts or superscripts of "n" denote coefficients in the canonical representation.

not all parameters in the above model can be identified. Singleton (2006) imposes identifying restrictions under the Q-measure. Specifically, he sets the mean θ_n^Q equal to zero, the volatility matrix Σ_n equal to the identity matrix, and the mean-reversion matrix K_n^Q equal to a triangular matrix.[15] The canonical representation is then

$$r_t = \delta_0^n + (\delta_1^n)' Y_t,$$

$$\begin{pmatrix} dY_t^1 \\ dY_t^2 \\ dY_t^3 \end{pmatrix} = \begin{pmatrix} \kappa_{11}^{n,P} & \kappa_{12}^{n,P} & \kappa_{13}^{n,P} \\ \kappa_{21}^{n,P} & \kappa_{22}^{n,P} & \kappa_{23}^{n,P} \\ \kappa_{31}^{n,P} & \kappa_{32}^{n,P} & \kappa_{33}^{n,P} \end{pmatrix} \left[\begin{pmatrix} \theta_1^{n,P} \\ \theta_2^{n,P} \\ \theta_3^{n,P} \end{pmatrix} - \begin{pmatrix} Y_t^1 \\ Y_t^2 \\ Y_t^3 \end{pmatrix} \right] dt$$
$$+ \begin{pmatrix} 1 & 0 & 0 \\ 0 & 1 & 0 \\ 0 & 0 & 1 \end{pmatrix} \begin{pmatrix} dW_t^{1,P} \\ dW_t^{2,P} \\ dW_t^{3,P} \end{pmatrix},$$

$$\begin{pmatrix} dY_t^1 \\ dY_t^2 \\ dY_t^3 \end{pmatrix} = - \begin{pmatrix} \kappa_{11}^{n,Q} & \kappa_{12}^{n,Q} & \kappa_{13}^{n,Q} \\ 0 & \kappa_{22}^{n,Q} & \kappa_{23}^{n,Q} \\ 0 & 0 & \kappa_{33}^{n,Q} \end{pmatrix} \begin{pmatrix} Y_t^1 \\ Y_t^2 \\ Y_t^3 \end{pmatrix} dt$$
$$+ \begin{pmatrix} 1 & 0 & 0 \\ 0 & 1 & 0 \\ 0 & 0 & 1 \end{pmatrix} \begin{pmatrix} dW_t^{1,Q} \\ dW_t^{2,Q} \\ dW_t^{3,Q} \end{pmatrix}.$$

Hence there are 22 free parameters in the canonical representation of the $A_0(3)$ model class.[16]

---

[15] Without loss of generality, in what follows we take the mean-reversion matrix K_n^Q to be upper triangular.

[16] Note that, given this canonical representation, there is no loss of generality in fixing the AFNS model mean under the Q-measure at 0 and leaving the mean under the P-measure, θ^P, to be estimated.

In the AFNS class, the mean-reversion matrix under the Q-measure is triangular, so it is straightforward to derive the restrictions on $A_0(3)$ that produce AFNS. We do so using affine invariant transformations, as described in Appendix B.

We summarize the results in Table 3.1. Correlated-factor AFNS puts three key parameter restrictions on $A_0(3)$. First, $\delta_0^n = 0$; that is, the instantaneous risk-free rate equation has no intercept. There is no need for an intercept because with the second restriction, $\kappa_{1,1}^{n,Q} = 0$, the first factor must be a unit-root process under the Q-measure, which also implies that this factor can be identified as the level factor. Finally, $\kappa_{2,2}^{n,Q} = \kappa_{3,3}^{n,Q}$; that is, the own mean-reversion rates of the second and third factors must be identical under the Q-measure. Independent-factor AFNS maintains the three correlated-factor AFNS parameter restrictions and adds nine more, six of which are restrictions under the P-measure and three of which are restrictions under the Q-measure.[17]

The Nelson-Siegel parameter restrictions on the canonical affine AF model greatly facilitate estimation. In the AFNS model, the connection between the P-dynamics and the yield function is explicitly tied to the yield-adjustment term through the specification of the volatility matrix, while in the canonical representation it is blurred by an interplay between the specifications of δ_1^n and K_n^Q. The Nelson-Siegel parameter restrictions allow a closed-form solution and, as described in the next section, eliminate in an appealing way the surfeit of troublesome likelihood maxima in estimation.

---

[17] For both AFNS specifications, there is a further modest restriction described in Appendix B: $\kappa_{2,3}^{n,Q}$ must have the opposite sign of $\kappa_{2,2}^{n,Q}$ and $\kappa_{3,3}^{n,Q}$, but its absolute numerical size can vary freely.

Table 3.1.   AFNS Parameter Restrictions on
the Canonical $A_0(3)$ Model

Restricted parameter	Independent-factor AFNS	Correlated-factor AFNS
$\delta_0^n,\ \delta_1^n$	$\delta_0^n = 0$ $\delta_{1,3}^n = 0$	$\delta_0^n = 0$ κ_n^Q
κ_n^Q	$\kappa_{1,1}^{n,Q} = \kappa_{1,2}^{n,Q} = \kappa_{1,3}^{n,Q} = 0$ $\kappa_{2,2}^{n,Q} = \kappa_{3,3}^{n,Q}$	$\kappa_{1,1}^{n,Q} = 0$ $\kappa_{2,2}^{n,Q} = \kappa_{3,3}^{n,Q}$
κ_n^P	κ_n^P diagonal	None
θ_n^P	None	None
Number of restrictions	12	3

3.6   Estimation

Thus far we have derived the affine arbitrage-free class of Nelson-Siegel term structure models, and we have explicitly characterized the restrictions that it places on the canonical $A_0(3)$ model. Here we show how to estimate the AFNS model using a Kalman filter–based maximum-likelihood approach. We first obtain the state-space representation of the AFNS model.

Recall that the DNS state transition and measurement equations are simply

$$X_t = (I - A)\mu + AX_{t-1} + \eta_t$$

and

$$y_t = BX_t + \varepsilon_t, \tag{3.16}$$

where $X_t = (L_t, S_t, C_t)$. The AFNS state-space representation is a bit trickier, as it needs to be converted from continuous to discrete time.

For continuous-time AFNS, the conditional mean vector is

$$E^P[X_T|\mathcal{F}_t] = (I - \exp(-K^P \Delta t))\theta^P + \exp(-K^P \Delta t)X_t$$

and the conditional covariance matrix is

$$V^P[X_T|\mathcal{F}_t] = \int_0^{\Delta t} e^{-K^P s} \Sigma\Sigma'^{-(K^P)'s} ds,$$

where $\Delta t = T - t$. The AFNS conditional mean expression implies that the AFNS state transition equation is

$$X_t = (I - \exp(-K^P \Delta t))\theta^P + \exp(-K^P \Delta t)X_{t-1} + \eta_t,$$

where Δt is the time between observations. Moreover, the conditional variance expression implies that the variance of the transition shock η_t is

$$Q = \int_0^{\Delta t} e^{-K^P s} \Sigma\Sigma'^{-(K^P)'s} ds.$$

Finally, the AFNS measurement equation is[18]

$$y_t = BX_t + C + \varepsilon_t.$$

In both the DNS and AFNS environments the stochastic disturbance structure is

$$\begin{pmatrix} \eta_t \\ \varepsilon_t \end{pmatrix} \sim N \left[\begin{pmatrix} 0 \\ 0 \end{pmatrix}, \begin{pmatrix} Q & 0 \\ 0 & H \end{pmatrix} \right],$$

---

[18] Note that the matrix B is identical in the DNS and AFNS models. The only difference is the addition of the vector C containing the yield-adjustment terms in the AFNS models.

where the matrix H is diagonal, and the matrix Q is diagonal in the independent-factor and nondiagonal in the correlated-factor case.[19]

Now we consider Kalman filtering, which we use to evaluate the likelihood functions of the DNS and AFNS models. We initialize the filter at the unconditional mean and variance of the state variables under the P-measure.[20] For the DNS models we have $X_0 = \mu$ and $\Sigma_0 = V$, where V solves $V = AVA' + Q$. For the AFNS models we have $X_0 = \theta^P$ and

$$\Sigma_0 = \int_0^\infty e^{-K^P s} \Sigma \Sigma'^{-(K^P)' s} ds,$$

which we calculate using the analytical solutions provided in Fisher and Gilles (1996).

Denote model parameters by ψ, and denote the information available at time t by $Y_t = (y_1, y_2, \ldots, y_t)$. Consider period $t - 1$ and suppose that the state update X_{t-1} and its mean square error matrix Σ_{t-1} have been obtained. The prediction step is

$$X_{t|t-1} = E^P[X_t|Y_{t-1}] = \Phi_t^{X,0}(\psi) + \Phi_t^{X,1}(\psi)X_{t-1},$$
$$\Sigma_{t|t-1} = \Phi_t^{X,1}(\psi)\Sigma_{t-1}\Phi_t^{X,1}(\psi)' + Q_t(\psi),$$

where for the DNS models we have

$$\Phi_t^{X,0} = (I - A)\mu,$$
$$\Phi_t^{X,1} = A,$$
$$Q_t = Q,$$

---

[19] We also assume that the transition and measurement errors are orthogonal to the initial state.

[20] We ensure covariance stationarity under the P-measure in the DNS case by restricting the eigenvalues of A to be less than 1, and in the AFNS case by restricting the real component of each eigenvalue of K^P to be positive.

and for the AFNS models we have

$$\Phi_t^{X,0} = (I - \exp(-K^P \Delta t))\theta^P,$$
$$\Phi_t^{X,1} = \exp(-K^P \Delta t),$$
$$Q_t = \int_0^{\Delta t} e^{-K^P s} \Sigma\Sigma'^{-(K^P)'s} ds,$$

where Δt is the time between observations.

Now consider the time-t update step, in which we improve $X_{t|t-1}$ by using the additional information contained in Y_t. We have

$$X_t = E[X_t|Y_t] = X_{t|t-1} + \Sigma_{t|t-1}B(\psi)'F_t^{-1}v_t,$$
$$\Sigma_t = \Sigma_{t|t-1} - \Sigma_{t|t-1}B(\psi)'F_t^{-1}B(\psi)\Sigma_{t|t-1},$$

where

$$v_t = y_t - E[y_t|Y_{t-1}] = y_t - B(\psi)X_{t|t-1} - C(\psi),$$
$$F_t = \text{cov}(v_t) = B(\psi)\Sigma_{t|t-1}B(\psi)' + H(\psi),$$
$$H(\psi) = \text{diag}(\sigma_\varepsilon^2(\tau_1), \ldots, \sigma_\varepsilon^2(\tau_N)).$$

The union of the above prediction and updating recursions is the Kalman filter.

A single pass of the Kalman filter delivers all ingredients needed to evaluate the Gaussian log likelihood, the prediction-error decomposition of which is

$$\log l(y_1, \ldots, y_T; \psi)$$
$$= \sum_{t=1}^T (-\tfrac{1}{2}N\log(2\pi) - \tfrac{1}{2}\log|F_t| - \tfrac{1}{2}v_t'F_t^{-1}v_t),$$

where N is the number of observed yields. We numerically maximize the likelihood with respect to ψ.

3.7   AFNS Fit and Forecasting

We have already sketched briefly some aspects of DNS fit and forecasting. Now we do the same for AFNS, beginning to ascertain, in particular, the fit and forecasting effects of imposition of no-arbitrage. The issues, however, are complicated and will be addressed not only here, but also in certain of the extensions in the next chapter, as well as in the epilogue (Chapter 6).

At some level it seems clear that, other things equal (and this *ceterus paribus* condition is crucial), imposition of no-arbitrage must degrade in-sample fit as it involves restrictions, and that it may or may not improve out-of-sample forecasting, again as it involves restrictions. On the other hand, as we have shown in detail, the AFNS *P*-measure restrictions are in a sense minimal, with no impact on dynamics, instead involving only a constant yield-adjustment term to account for Jensen's inequality effects. Similarly, it seems clear that, *ceterus paribus*, the independent-factor models must fit worse than correlated-factor models but may or may not forecast better.

These assertions accord with the empirical findings of Christensen et al. (2011a), who examine AFNS in-sample fit and out-of-sample forecast performance relative to DNS (for both independent-factor and correlated-factor versions). As regards in-sample fit, they show that the Nelson-Siegel parameter restrictions greatly facilitate estimation, enabling one to escape the challenging $A_0(3)$ estimation environment in favor of the simple and robust AFNS environment, and that the data strongly favor the

Table 3.2. Out-of-Sample Forecasting Performance: Four DNS and AFNS Models

Model	Forecast Horizon (months)	
	$h = 6$	$h = 12$
3-Month Yield		
DNS_{indep}	96.87	173.39
DNS_{corr}	87.43	166.91
AFNS_{indep}	91.63	164.70
AFNS_{corr}	88.49	161.94
1-Year Yield		
DNS_{indep}	103.25	170.85
DNS_{corr}	102.71	173.14
AFNS_{indep}	98.49	163.46
AFNS_{corr}	98.63	165.50
3-Year Yield		
DNS_{indep}	92.22	135.24
DNS_{corr}	99.55	145.82
AFNS_{indep}	86.99	126.95
AFNS_{corr}	90.64	135.79
5-Year Yield		
DNS_{indep}	87.87	122.09
DNS_{corr}	94.95	132.40
AFNS_{indep}	82.41	112.85
AFNS_{corr}	88.15	124.87
10-Year Yield		
DNS_{indep}	74.71	105.02
DNS_{corr}	79.48	112.37
AFNS_{indep}	67.48	92.39
AFNS_{corr}	90.21	123.89

Notes: We show out-of-sample root mean squared forecast errors for each of four models. For each maturity and horizon, the smallest RMSFE is boxed. Units are basis points.

Table 3.3.   Out-of-Sample Forecasting Performance:
Random Walk, $A_0(3)$, and AFNS$_{indep}$

Maturity/Model	Forecast Horizon (months)	
	$h = 6$	$h = 12$
6-Month Yield		
Random walk	40.0	48.4
Preferred $A_0(3)$	36.5	42.1
AFNS$_{indep}$	34.0	41.3
2-Year Yield		
Random walk	65.2	76.2
Preferred $A_0(3)$	56.6	60.0
AFNS$_{indep}$	54.3	59.0
10-Year Yield		
Random walk	66.9	81.5
Preferred $A_0(3)$	63.6	73.8
AFNS$_{indep}$	60.7	71.8

Notes: We show RMSFEs for the random walk model, Duffee's preferred $A_0(3)$ model, and the independent-factor AFNS
model estimated using Duffee's data set. For each maturity
and horizon, the smallest RMSFE is boxed. Units are basis
points. For details see Christensen et al. (2011a).

more-flexible correlated-factor specifications, whether for
DNS or for AFNS.

As regards out-of-sample prediction, Christensen et al.
(2011a) show that the tables are turned: The more parsimonious independent-factor models fare better. Moreover, and of great interest, they find that gains are often
achieved by imposing absence of arbitrage within each
model class (independent-factor, correlated-factor), particularly for the independent-factor model. Table 3.2
nicely summarizes the predictive results. AFNS$_{indep}$ is

the winner for 9 of 10 forecasting competitions (five maturities, two forecast horizons). In addition, several comparisons are of interest: AFNS_{corr} vs. AFNS_{indep} (AFNS_{indep} is the clear winner), DNS_{corr} vs. AFNS_{corr} (mixed results), DNS_{corr} vs. DNS_{indep} (mixed results but generally favoring DNS_{indep}). In our view, the penultimate comparison is DNS_{indep} vs. AFNS_{indep}, as we and others have always stressed the independent-factor model, and within that model we want to see the predictive effects of imposing absence of arbitrage. The verdict is clear: AFNS_{indep} consistently beats DNS_{indep}.

We are hardly the first to find that imposition of no-arbitrage may improve yield curve forecasts. For example, Ang and Piazzesi (2003), Favero et al. (2011), and Mönch (2008) find that imposition of no-arbitrage often helps to improve forecasts in vector autoregressive models, as do Almeida and Vicente (2008) in polynomial models and Carriero and Giacomini (2011) when using economic loss functions. Moreover, we are certainly not alone in finding that AFNS_{indep} outperforms DNS_{indep} in out-of-sample forecasting. Indeed authors such as Gimeno and Marqués (2009), performing exactly the same sorts of DNS vs. AFNS comparisons as Christensen et al. (2011a), but on different data sets, find that imposition of no-arbitrage produces often huge forecast improvements.

Nevertheless, despite the evidence from us and others, the predictive enhancement from imposition of no-arbitrage on DNS is somewhat curious—perhaps even unsettling—insofar as our key Propositions AFNS and AFNS-adj make clear that freedom from arbitrage does not restrict physical yield dynamics. Recent work in more general contexts, such as Duffee (2011b), Joslin et al. (2011b), and Joslin et al. (2011a), arrives at a similarly pessimistic outlook regarding the likelihood of forecast improvement from imposition of no-arbitrage.

At least two possible explanations arise. First, working against our finding of predictive superiority of AFNS vs. DNS, we and various others may have simply been "lucky" regarding predictive outcomes on specific and often small samples. Certainly not *all* researchers have found predictive gains from imposing no-arbitrage. For example, Coroneo et al. (2011) and Nyholm and Vidova-Koleva (2011) evaluate empirically the merits of various approaches and conclude that models that fail to impose no-arbitrage are nevertheless often highly competitive for forecasting. That is, they find that imposing no-arbitrage adds little.

Second, working in favor of our finding of predictive superiority of AFNS vs. DNS, although no-arbitrage places no restrictions on DNS physical dynamics, it *does* add a potentially important yield-adjustment term, notwithstanding its time constancy. It is conceivable that the yield-adjustment term delivers substantial predictive gains of a "bias correction" type.

In the epilogue we return to the issue of predictive enhancement from imposition of no-arbitrage. Indeed we view increased understanding of whether and when imposition of no-arbitrage enhances forecasts as a leading item on the research agenda. For now, however, let us put that aside, not comparing the "arb" (DNS) vs. "no-arb" (AFNS) versions of our model, but rather comparing AFNS to another leading no-arbitrage model.

Particularly revealing is direct forecast comparison of independent-factor AFNS to an $A_0(3)$ model, as painstakingly selected, estimated, and used by a leading researcher. To that end, Christensen et al. (2011a) build on Duffee (2002), who examines the predictive performance of the $A_0(3)$ model class, estimating both the maximally flexible version (given essentially affine risk premium structure) and more parsimonious "preferred" specifications, January 1952 to December 1994. Christensen et al. extend Duffee's forecast comparison to include the independent-factor AFNS model, estimated using 3-month, 6-month, 1-year, 2-year, 5-year, and 10-year yields, using precisely Duffee's data set. There are 21 parameters to be estimated in Duffee's preferred $A_0(3)$ model and 16 parameters to be estimated in our AFNS model, including the six measurement error standard deviations.

RMSFEs appear in Table 3.3 for the two models examined by Duffee (2002) (random walk and $A_0(3)$) plus the independent-factor AFNS model, for the 6-month, 2-year and 10-year yield maturities examined by Duffee. RMSFEs for each forecasting model are based on 42 six-month-ahead forecasts from January 1995 to June 1998, and 36 twelve-month-ahead forecasts from January 1995 to December 1997. For each maturity–horizon combination, the independent-factor AFNS forecasts are the most accurate, consistently outperforming both the random walk and Duffee's preferred $A_0(3)$ model. This superior out-of-sample forecast performance clearly shows that independent-factor AFNS is a leading and, not least, well-identified member of the general $A_0(3)$ model class.

4

Extensions

In this chapter, we highlight aspects of the vibrant ongoing research program associated with the ideas developed in earlier chapters. We begin with a collage-style sketch of work involving Bayesian analysis, functional form for factor loadings, term structures of credit spreads, and nonlinearities. We then discuss in greater detail a time-honored topic that has received attention both historically and presently, incorporation of more than three yield factors. Third, we treat stochastic volatility in both DNS and AFNS environments, with some attention to the issue of unspanned stochastic volatility. Finally, we also discuss in detail a crucially important topic for the emerging research agenda, the incorporation of macroeconomic fundamentals in their relation to bond yields. Related, we introduce aspects of modeling real versus nominal yields in DNS/AFNS environments, a theme that we treat in detail in Chapter 5.

4.1   Variations on the Basic Theme

DNS/AFNS research is moving forward at a steady pace. Here we sketch a few of the more interesting and important developments, to convey a feel for the issues and ideas, and to provide relevant references for those who want to dig deeper.

4.1.1 Bayesian Shrinkage

Thus far we have either imposed various constraints, or we have not. Examples include the independence constraints associated with independent-factor DNS, the no-arbitrage constraints associated with correlated-factor AFNS, or the simultaneous imposition of both as in independent-factor AFNS.

One can think of such "hard constraints" as the outcome of a Bayesian analysis with spiked priors. But one may want to impose "soft constraints," coaxing ("shrinking") estimates in certain directions without forcing them. That is, one may want to do an informative-prior Bayesian analysis, but with less-than-perfect prior precision, so that likelihood information is blended with prior information rather than simply discarded. As is well-known, such shrinkage often improves forecasts.[1]

There is ample opportunity to use shrinkage ideas in predictive yield curve modeling, and research along those lines is appearing. Carriero et al. (2010) perform a Bayesian analysis of a vector autoregression for a large set of yields, using the "Minnesota prior" popular in the empirical macroeconomics literature.[2] They obtain encouraging forecasting results, systematically beating random walk forecasts, although not by much.

The Minnesota prior is a statistical prior. The obvious benchmark *economic* shrinkage direction for a yield curve model, however, is toward the restrictions implied by absence of arbitrage. Carriero (2011) does just that, shrinking but not forcing a vector autoregression toward the no-arbitrage configuration of Ang and Piazzesi (2003), with striking results. Forecasts based on

---

[1] See, for example, Diebold (2007).

[2] For discussion of the Minnesota prior, see the classic Doan et al. (1984).

vector autoregressions shrunken toward Ang-Piazzesi no-arbitrage improve on unrestricted vector-autoregressive forecasts, *and* on Ang-Piazzesi restricted vector-autoregressive forecasts, *and* on vector-autoregressive forecasts shrunken in other directions. In particular, forecasts from Ang-Piazzesi shrunken vector autoregressions dominate those from vector–random walk shrunken vector autoregressions associated with the Minnesota prior, especially at long horizons.[3]

An obvious remaining question is whether shrinkage toward the restrictions associated with AFNS, as opposed to strict imposition of those restrictions, would enhance the predictive performance of AFNS. On the one hand, as we have emphasized, shrinkage is often better than either unconstrained or completely constrained approaches. On the other hand, as we have also emphasized, the AFNS restrictions on DNS are actually quite minor and likely to hold quite closely even when not imposed or shrunken toward. We look forward to research that will resolve this tension.

Related, some preliminary evidence suggests possible gains from shrinking toward the strong Q-measure restrictions (as opposed to minimal P-measure restrictions) associated with AFNS. To the extent that the market is not risk-neutral, the Q-measure restrictions are not likely to hold exactly in the physical world, but at the same time they might not be too far off, and Hua (2010a) suggests that they may hold quite well. The empirical success of univariate orthogonal factor dynamics is potentially closely related. It corresponds to imposition of a diagonal dynamic matrix, but the risk-neutral

---

[3] Interestingly, recent results in empirical macroeconomics in the tradition of Ingram and Whiteman (1994) also find extra enhancement when shrinking in economically relevant directions. In particular, see Schorfheide (2011).

dynamic matrix *is* diagonal, apart from a single nonzero off-diagonal (2,3) element.

4.1.2 Alternative Factor Loadings

Yield factor loadings can be approached using parametric forms different from DNS. In an important early paper motivated by DNS, for example, Almeida (2005) seeks a model with interpretable factor structure that is also arbitrage-free. He models the term structure as a linear combination of Legendre polynomials with random coefficients and shows that it can indeed be made arbitrage-free. Thus, although Almeida's approach is mathematically very different from AFNS (polynomial loadings rather than "exponentials × polynomials"), it is quite similar in spirit.[4]

Alternatively, it is also possible to take a nonparametric approach to factor loadings. Park et al. (2009), for example, use a series estimation approach, and Fengler et al. (2007) use a kernel estimation approach.[5] Bowsher and Meeks (2008), Jungbacker et al. (2010), and Almeida et al. (2011) use cubic splines.

We emphasize, however, that relaxing parametric constraints is not necessarily desirable. Indeed the motivation for DNS and AFNS is that the unrestricted yield curve models generally lead to in-sample overfitting, so that imposing restrictions can be positively *helpful* and need not degrade fit substantially.[6] Hence if

---

[4] See also Almeida et al. (2003) and Almeida and Vicente (2008).

[5] Fengler et al. (2007) in turn build on Fengler et al. (2002) in both methodology and focus on implied volatility surfaces, so that the object modeled is a time series of three-dimensional *surfaces*. See also Brüggemann et al. (2008).

[6] For an interesting recent example of an exceptionally tightly parametric arbitrage-free yield curve model that nevertheless also fits exceptionally well, see Calvet et al. (2010).

nonparametric approaches are to be helpful, especially for out-of-sample prediction, they will likely need to be tuned to produce smooth loadings, like DNS.[7] In all cases, smoothness can be enforced as desired via appropriate bandwidth choice, although the "appropriate" bandwidth can be difficult to determine in practice.

One can also parameterize discount and forward rate curves in ways similar to DNS.[8] Two leading examples are Chua et al. (2008), who model the forward rate curve $f_t(\tau)$ using exponential components (whereas DNS of course models the *yield* curve $y_t(\tau)$ using exponential components), and Litzenberger et al. (1995), who model the discount curve $P_t(\tau)$ using exponential components.

Both the similarities and the differences of Litzenberger et al. (1995) relative to DNS are intriguing. The discount curve and the yield curve are related by a logarithmic transformation,

$$y_t(\tau) = -\frac{1}{\tau}\log P_t(\tau),$$

so the Litzenberger et al. and DNS approaches are equivalent in the one-factor case. In the multifactor case, however, a sum of factors in the yield curve will not be a sum in the discount curve (the log of a sum is not the sum of the logs), so there is generally no simple mapping between the two approaches.

4.1.3   Yield Spreads

Nelson-Siegel yield curves are closed under conversion to spreads. That is, if two term structures of yields $y_t^1(\tau)$

---

[7] This "smoothness prior" tradition traces at least to Shiller (1973). Jungbacker et al. (2010) and Almeida et al. (2011) progress in that direction by using different devices to promote smoothness.

[8] One could also use nonexponential parametric functional approximations, as well as nonparametric approaches, in both the discount and forward rate curve environments.

and $y_t^2(\tau)$ follow DNS with the same λ, then the term structure of *spreads* also follows DNS. In particular, if

$$y_t^1(\tau) = l_t^1 + s_t^1 \left(\frac{1 - e^{\lambda\tau}}{\lambda\tau}\right) + c_t^1 \left(\frac{1 - e^{\lambda\tau}}{\lambda\tau} - e^{-\lambda\tau}\right)$$

and

$$y_t^2(\tau) = l_t^2 + s_t^2 \left(\frac{1 - e^{\lambda\tau}}{\lambda\tau}\right) + c_t^2 \left(\frac{1 - e^{\lambda\tau}}{\lambda\tau} - e^{-\lambda\tau}\right),$$

then trivial algebra reveals that

$$dy_t(\tau) = dl_t + ds_t \left(\frac{1 - e^{\lambda\tau}}{\lambda\tau}\right) + dc_t \left(\frac{1 - e^{\lambda\tau}}{\lambda\tau} - e^{-\lambda\tau}\right),$$

where

$$dy_t(\tau) = (y_t^1(\tau) - y_t^2(\tau)),$$
$$dl_t = (l_t^1 - l_t^2),$$
$$ds_t = (s_t^1 - s_t^2),$$
$$dc_t = (c_t^1 - c_t^2).$$

Note the intuitive result that each spread curve factor is just the difference of the corresponding underlying yield curve factors.

Closure under conversion to spreads is useful in applications, as term structures of spreads are often of interest. Chen and Tsang (2009, 2010), for example, use DNS models to study the term structure of cross-country government bond spreads, which by covered interest parity is equivalent to the term structure of forward premia.[9] In a study of the United States, United Kingdom, Canada, and Japan, they find that the spread curve factors have predictive content for future bilateral spot exchange rates at horizons ranging from 1 to 24 months.

---

[9] See also Koivu et al. (2007a,b).

Term structures of corporate bond spreads (spreads of defaultable corporate bond yields of a given grade against risk-free government bond yields) are also of great interest. Yu and Salyards (2009) and Yu and Zivot (2011), for example, use DNS to forecast investment-grade and speculative-grade corporate bonds from December 1994 to April 2006.[10] They obtain good forecasts using standard independent-factor DNS, and they document substantial differences in extracted factor dynamics for investment-grade versus speculative-grade bonds. Christensen and Lopez (2011) use the arbitrage-free version of DNS (AFNS) to examine whether U.S. corporate bond spread factors have predictive content for Treasury yields. In Christensen et al. (2010b) they use that same model to investigate the effect of central bank liquidity facilities on term interbank lending rates.

In the most ambitious DNS-style spread modeling to date, Hua (2010b) works in the "Merton model" tradition of Merton (1974) and Campbell and Tacksler (2003), relating corporate bond spreads to equity volatilities. He works with entire term structures, however, relating yield-spread term-structure factors to equity-market implied volatility term-structure factors, with each of the term structures fit using DNS. Hua finds strong evidence that the volatility factors, especially the volatility level factor, Granger-causes credit spread levels, confirming the theoretical predictions of Merton (1974) in a significantly richer and more nuanced environment than previously entertained.

4.1.4 Nonlinearities

Nonlinearities arise in a variety of shapes and sizes. Here we focus on two. First we entertain time-varying λ, which

---

[10] See also Krishnan et al. (2010).

moves us from a linear to a nonlinear state-space environment. Second, we entertain regime-switching yield factor dynamics.

4.1.4.1 Time-varying λ

One can allow for time-varying λ in estimation. The measurement equation (2.3) now involves a time-varying system matrix of factor loadings,

$$y_t = \Lambda_t f_t + \varepsilon_t, \tag{4.1}$$

where

$$\Lambda_t = \begin{pmatrix} 1 & \dfrac{1 - e^{-\tau_1 \lambda_t}}{\tau_1 \lambda_t} & \dfrac{1 - e^{-\tau_1 \lambda_t}}{\tau_1 \lambda_t} - e^{-\tau_1 \lambda_t} \\ 1 & \dfrac{1 - e^{-\tau_2 \lambda_t}}{\tau_2 \lambda_t} & \dfrac{1 - e^{-\tau_2 \lambda_t}}{\tau_2 \lambda_t} - e^{-\tau_2 \lambda_t} \\ \vdots & \vdots & \vdots \\ 1 & \dfrac{1 - e^{-\tau_N \lambda_t}}{\tau_N \lambda_t} & \dfrac{1 - e^{-\tau_N \lambda_t}}{\tau_N \lambda_t} - e^{-\tau_N \lambda_t} \end{pmatrix}.$$

We also add λ_t to the state vector to incorporate its dynamics.

Models of this sort are explored by Koopman et al. (2010a). They could be particularly useful in situations that involve not only time-varying curvature (as always), but also time-varying location of maximal curvature ("bow center"). Recently, for example, a significant and changing part of the short end of the U.S. yield curve has been at the zero bound. Time-varying λ may help capture such time-varying yield curve kinks.

Counterbalancing the potential appeal of time-varying λ sketched here, however, is the fact that AFNS as presently developed invokes constant λ. Whether constancy of λ, together with the other AFNS assumptions, is *necessary* for no-arbitrage remains an open question, and we look forward to additional research.

4.1.4.2 Regime-switching state dynamics

DNS has been significantly enriched by several authors to include nonlinear regime-switching yield factor dynamics. In all cases the basic idea is to replace linear yield factor dynamics,

$$f_t = c + A f_{t-1} + \eta_t,$$

with regime-switching dynamics along the lines of

$$f_t = c_{s_t} + A_{s_t} f_{t-1} + \eta_t,$$
$$\eta_t \sim N(0, \sigma_{s_t}^2),$$

where $s_t = 1, 2$ in the leading case of a two-state model. The standard linear dynamics emerge as a special case when $c_1 = c_2$, $A_1 = A_2$ and $\sigma_1^2 = \sigma_2^2$.

For example, Bernadell et al. (2005) allow for Markov regime-switching dynamics in the tradition of Hamilton (1989), in which case s_t is a latent first-order Markov process. Indeed they go even further, allowing for a time-varying transition-probability matrix in the tradition of Diebold et al. (1994). Hence s_t is governed by[11]

$$P_t = \begin{pmatrix} p_{11,t} & 1 - p_{11,t} \\ 1 - p_{22,t} & p_{22,t} \end{pmatrix}.$$

Zantedeschi et al. (2011) work in a related nonlinear non-Gaussian environment, using a particle filter for inference. Indeed recent advances in sequential Monte

---

[11] See also Nyholm (2008), Nyholm and Rebonato (2008), and Guidolin and Timmermann (2009).

Carlo methods open the door for unified analysis and estimation of very general nonlinear and non-Gaussian state-space yield curve models.[12]

4.2 Additional Yield Factors

Occasionally in the DNS literature one sees two-factor models; that is, curvature is omitted. This is typically done, however, for tractability rather than realism, as in the early multicountry model of Diebold et al. (2008) and the two-factor AFNS precursor of Diebold et al. (2005). Indeed much more attention has focused on inclusion of *additional* factors.

Foremost among such models with additional factors is the Svensson (1995) extension of the Nelson-Siegel curve, which is widely used in industry and central banks.[13] Svensson adds a second curvature variable with a longer-maturity hump, thereby promoting better fit at longer maturities. Hence we now proceed to dynamize the Svensson model. Several surprises await.

4.2.1 Four Factors: Dynamic Nelson-Siegel-Svensson (DNSS)

The Nelson-Siegel slope and curvature variables rapidly approach zero with maturity. Hence only the level is available to fit long-maturity yields (roughly 10 years or longer). To address this occasional problem in fitting the cross section of yields, Svensson (1995) introduced

---

[12] See, for example, Fulop (2009) and Giordani et al. (2011).

[13] Examples include the U.S. Federal Reserve Board (see Gürkaynak et al. (2007)), the European Central Bank (see Coroneo et al. (2011)), and many other central banks (see Söderlind and Svensson (1997) and BIS (2005)).

an extended version of Nelson-Siegel with an additional curvature variable,

$$y(\tau) = \beta_1 + \beta_2 \left(\frac{1 - e^{-\lambda_1 \tau}}{\lambda_1 \tau} \right) + \beta_3 \left(\frac{1 - e^{-\lambda_1 \tau}}{\lambda_1 \tau} - e^{-\lambda_1 \tau} \right)$$
$$+ \beta_4 \left(\frac{1 - e^{-\lambda_2 \tau}}{\lambda_2 \tau} - e^{-\lambda_2 \tau} \right).$$

As expected, in empirical fitting to cross sections of yields, the Svensson extension often fits better than NS at long maturities.

Just as Diebold and Li (2006) replaced the three β coefficients with dynamic processes ("factors") in the Nelson-Siegel model, we can replace the four β coefficients in the Nelson-Siegel-Svensson model with dynamic processes (L_t, S_t, C_t^1, C_t^2) interpreted as level, slope, first curvature, and second curvature factors, respectively. This dynamic factor version of the Nelson-Siegel-Svensson curve, which we call the dynamic Nelson-Siegel-Svensson (DNSS), is

$$y_t(\tau) = L_t + S_t \left(\frac{1 - e^{-\lambda_1 \tau}}{\lambda_1 \tau} \right) + C_t^1 \left(\frac{1 - e^{-\lambda_1 \tau}}{\lambda_1 \tau} - e^{-\lambda_1 \tau} \right)$$
$$+ C_t^2 \left(\frac{1 - e^{-\lambda_2 \tau}}{\lambda_2 \tau} - e^{-\lambda_2 \tau} \right).$$

We show the four factor loadings as functions of maturity in Figure 4.1. Completion of the DNSS model requires specification of factor dynamics, which we take as a vector autoregression, just as in DNS.

The Filipović (1999) critique of NS, namely that it would not be arbitrage-free if dynamized, also applies to the four-factor DNSS model just introduced. One would

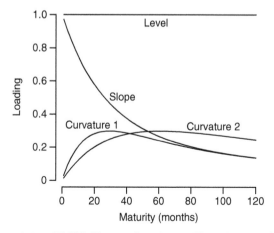

Figure 4.1. DNSS Factor Loadings. We plot DNSS factor loadings as a function of maturity, for $\lambda_1 = 0.0609$ and $\lambda_2 = 0.0295$.

hope that, in parallel to AFNS and DNS, one could derive an arbitrage-free approximation to DNSS. However, as the mechanics of Proposition AFNS of Chapter 3 make clear, an arbitrage-free Gaussian version of DNSS cannot exist, because it would require that each curvature factor be paired with a slope factor with the same rate of mean reversion, which is impossible with the single slope factor present in DNSS.[14] Hence in the next subsection we add a second slope factor to match Svensson's second curvature factor, and we ask whether risk-neutral restrictions can be found that make the five-factor model arbitrage-free.

---

[14] It is technically possible, however, to create an arbitrage-free version of DNSS if one leaves the Gaussian class, as in the model of Sharef and Filipović (2004), which has Cox et al. (1985) square-root volatility.

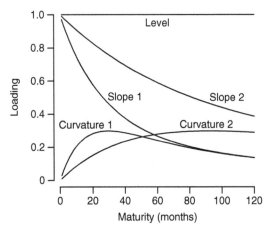

Figure 4.2. DGNS Factor Loadings. We plot DGNS factor loadings as a function of maturity, for $\lambda_1 = 0.0609$ and $\lambda_2 = 0.0295$.

4.2.2 Five Factors: Arbitrage-Free Generalized Nelson-Siegel (AFGNS)

The preceding discussion suggests that we can create a generalized AFNS model by including a fifth factor in the form of a second slope factor. Following Christensen et al. (2009), the yield function of this model takes the form

$$
\begin{aligned}
y_t(\tau) = L_t + S_t^1 \left(\frac{1 - e^{-\lambda_1 \tau}}{\lambda_1 \tau} \right) + S_t^2 \left(\frac{1 - e^{-\lambda_2 \tau}}{\lambda_2 \tau} \right) \\
+ C_t^1 \left(\frac{1 - e^{-\lambda_1 \tau}}{\lambda_1 \tau} - e^{-\lambda_1 \tau} \right) \\
+ C_t^2 \left(\frac{1 - e^{-\lambda_2 \tau}}{\lambda_2 \tau} - e^{-\lambda_2 \tau} \right).
\end{aligned}
$$

This dynamic generalized Nelson-Siegel model, which we denote as the DGNS model, is a five-factor model with one level factor, two slope factors, and two curvature factors. Note that we impose the restriction that $\lambda_1 > \lambda_2$, which is nonbinding due to symmetry.[15] We show the five factor loadings as functions of maturity in Figure 4.2.

A straightforward extension of Proposition AFNS delivers the arbitrage-free version of the DGNS model, which we call the arbitrage-free generalized Nelson-Siegel model.

Proposition (Proposition AFGNS). *Assume that the instantaneous risk-free rate is given by*

$$r_t = X_t^1 + X_t^2 + X_t^3,$$

and assume that the five state variables X_t^1, X_t^2, X_t^3, X_t^4, X_t^5 are described by the SDEs under the risk-neutral Q-measure:

$$
\begin{pmatrix} dX_t^1 \\ dX_t^2 \\ dX_t^3 \\ dX_t^4 \\ dX_t^5 \end{pmatrix} =
\begin{pmatrix}
0 & 0 & 0 & 0 & 0 \\
0 & \lambda_1 & 0 & -\lambda_1 & 0 \\
0 & 0 & \lambda_2 & 0 & -\lambda_2 \\
0 & 0 & 0 & \lambda_1 & 0 \\
0 & 0 & 0 & 0 & \lambda_2
\end{pmatrix}
$$

$$
\times \left(\begin{pmatrix} \theta_1^Q \\ \theta_2^Q \\ \theta_3^Q \\ \theta_4^Q \\ \theta_5^Q \end{pmatrix} - \begin{pmatrix} X_t^1 \\ X_t^2 \\ X_t^3 \\ X_t^4 \\ X_t^5 \end{pmatrix} \right) dt + \Sigma \begin{pmatrix} dW_t^{1,Q} \\ dW_t^{2,Q} \\ dW_t^{3,Q} \\ dW_t^{4,Q} \\ dW_t^{5,Q} \end{pmatrix},
$$

---

[15] Björk and Christensen (1999) introduce a related extension of the Nelson-Siegel model with one level factor, two slope factors, and a single curvature factor with the restriction that $\lambda_1 = 2\lambda_2$.

where $\lambda_1 > \lambda_2 > 0$. Then zero-coupon bond prices are

$$P(t,T) = E_t^Q \left(\exp\left(-\int_t^T r_u du \right) \right)$$
$$= \exp(B^1(t,T)X_t^1 + B^2(t,T)X_t^2 + B^3(t,T)X_t^3$$
$$+ B^4(t,T)X_t^4 + B^5(t,T)X_t^5 + C(t,T)),$$

where $B^1(t,T)$, $B^2(t,T)$, $B^3(t,T)$, $B^4(t,T)$, $B^5(t,T)$, and $C(t,T)$ are the unique solutions to the system of ODEs:

$$\begin{pmatrix} \dfrac{dB^1(t,T)}{dt} \\[2mm] \dfrac{dB^2(t,T)}{dt} \\[2mm] \dfrac{dB^3(t,T)}{dt} \\[2mm] \dfrac{dB^4(t,T)}{dt} \\[2mm] \dfrac{dB^5(t,T)}{dt} \end{pmatrix}$$
$$= \begin{pmatrix} 1 \\ 1 \\ 1 \\ 0 \\ 0 \end{pmatrix} + \begin{pmatrix} 0 & 0 & 0 & 0 & 0 \\ 0 & \lambda_1 & 0 & 0 & 0 \\ 0 & 0 & \lambda_2 & 0 & 0 \\ 0 & -\lambda_1 & 0 & \lambda_1 & 0 \\ 0 & 0 & -\lambda_2 & 0 & \lambda_2 \end{pmatrix} \begin{pmatrix} B^1(t,T) \\ B^2(t,T) \\ B^3(t,T) \\ B^4(t,T) \\ B^5(t,T) \end{pmatrix}$$

and

$$\frac{dC(t,T)}{dt} = -B(t,T)'^Q \theta^Q - \frac{1}{2} \sum_{j=1}^5 \left(\Sigma' B(t,T) B(t,T)' \Sigma \right)_{j,j},$$

with boundary conditions $B^1(T,T) = B^2(T,T) = B^3(T,T) = B^4(T,T) = B^5(T,T) = C(T,T) = 0$.

The unique solution for this system of ODEs is

$$B^1(t,T) = -(T-t),$$

$$B^2(t,T) = -\frac{1-e^{-\lambda_1(T-t)}}{\lambda_1},$$

$$B^3(t,T) = -\frac{1-e^{-\lambda_2(T-t)}}{\lambda_2},$$

$$B^4(t,T) = (T-t)e^{-\lambda_1(T-t)} - \frac{1-e^{-\lambda_1(T-t)}}{\lambda_1},$$

$$B^5(t,T) = (T-t)e^{-\lambda_2(T-t)} - \frac{1-e^{-\lambda_2(T-t)}}{\lambda_2},$$

and

$$
\begin{aligned}
C(t,T) = {}& (K^Q\theta^Q)_2 \int_t^T B^2(s,T)ds \\
& + (K^Q\theta^Q)_3 \int_t^T B^3(s,T)ds \\
& + (K^Q\theta^Q)_4 \int_t^T B^4(s,T)ds \\
& + (K^Q\theta^Q)_5 \int_t^T B^5(s,T)ds \\
& + \frac{1}{2}\sum_{j=1}^5 \int_t^T \left(\Sigma' B(s,T)B(s,T)'\Sigma\right)_{j,j}ds.
\end{aligned}
$$

Finally, zero-coupon bond yields are

$$
\begin{aligned}
y(t,T) = {}& X_t^1 + \frac{1-e^{-\lambda_1(T-t)}}{\lambda_1(T-t)}X_t^2 + \frac{1-e^{-\lambda_2(T-t)}}{\lambda_2(T-t)}X_t^3 \\
& + \left(\frac{1-e^{-\lambda_1(T-t)}}{\lambda_1(T-t)} - e^{-\lambda_1(T-t)}\right)X_t^4 \\
& + \left(\frac{1-e^{-\lambda_2(T-t)}}{\lambda_2(T-t)} - e^{-\lambda_2(T-t)}\right)X_t^5 - \frac{C(t,T)}{T-t}.
\end{aligned}
$$

Proof. This is a straightforward extension of Proposition AFNS.   □

In similar fashion to the AFNS class of models, the yield-adjustment term has the form[16]

$$-\frac{C(t,T)}{T-t} = -\frac{1}{2}\frac{1}{T-t}\sum_{j=1}^{5}\int_{t}^{T}\left(\Sigma' B(s,T)B(s,T)'\Sigma\right)_{j,j}ds,$$

and the maximally flexible specification of the volatility matrix that can be identified in estimation is given by a triangular matrix

$$\Sigma = \begin{pmatrix} \sigma_{11} & 0 & 0 & 0 & 0 \\ \sigma_{21} & \sigma_{22} & 0 & 0 & 0 \\ \sigma_{31} & \sigma_{32} & \sigma_{33} & 0 & 0 \\ \sigma_{41} & \sigma_{42} & \sigma_{43} & \sigma_{44} & 0 \\ \sigma_{51} & \sigma_{52} & \sigma_{53} & \sigma_{54} & \sigma_{55} \end{pmatrix}.$$

4.2.3 Discussion

Christensen et al. (2009) develop and empirically explore the DNSS, DGNS, and AFGNS models. De Pooter (2007) finds some evidence for more than three factors; in particular, he obtains improved fit and prediction with a four-factor model. Almeida et al. (2009) propose a four-factor model and argue that it outperforms the Diebold and Li (2006) three-factor model in a forecasting competition on Brazilian data. Fontaine and Garcia (2008) include a fourth factor that captures liquidity.

---

[16] We provide the analytical formula for the AFGNS yield-adjustment term in Appendix C. As was the case for Proposition AFNS, Proposition AFGNS is also silent regarding the P-dynamics of the state variables, so to identify the model, we follow Christensen et al. (2011a) and fix the mean under the Q-measure at zero, i.e., $\theta^{Q} = 0$.

Cochrane and Piazzesi (2005) use a fourth factor that is a tent-shaped weighted average of forward rates, which they argue has strong predictive content. Wei and Wright (2010) argue that the Cochrane-Piazzesi predictability claim is suspect, due to faulty econometrics. Related, Duffee (2010) shows that the Cochrane-Piazzesi result implies existence of a trading strategy with a preposterously large Sharpe ratio.

Some recent work uses more than four factors: Both Duffee (2010) and Joslin et al. (2009) use five. One could imagine models with even larger numbers of factors, and large numbers of factors may sometimes be relevant. The striking and important point, however, is that low-dimensional (e.g., three-dimensional) factor structure is typically adequate.

4.3   Stochastic Volatility

As with most asset returns, bond yields or returns tend to display time-varying volatility, or conditional heteroskedasticity, as well as the corresponding fat-tailed, or leptokurtic, unconditional distributions. This is particularly true when yields are measured at high frequency, such as daily, as is often the case.

The necessity or desirability of incorporating stochastic volatility into the transition or measurement shocks depends on the envisioned use of the model. For point forecasting with a reasonably large sample, for example, stochastic volatility can probably be ignored at the cost of only a small reduction in estimation efficiency. On the other hand, if interest centers on interval or density forecasts of yields or yield factors, then stochastic volatility is of direct and intrinsic interest and cannot be ignored.

4.3.1   DNS Formulation

Interestingly, in the DNS state-space formulation (2.3)–
(2.4), stochastic volatility could enter through the measurement shocks or the transition shocks, and different
possibilities have been considered by different authors.
Koopman et al. (2010a) and Laurini and Hotta (2010),
for example, allow for stochastic volatility in the measurement shocks using the single-factor multivariate
GARCH model of Harvey et al. (1992). Alternatively,
Hautsch and Ou (2008) and Hautsch and Yang (2010)
allow for stochastic volatility in the transition equation.
They find strong evidence of stochastic volatility in the
transition shocks, particularly for level and slope, and
they show that accounting for it improves the conditional
calibration of interval and density forecasts.

Our preference runs toward allowing stochastic volatility in the transition equation, as the transition dynamics characterize the deep workings of the system, and
moreover that approach is potentially simpler to imple-
ment, as the dimension of the yield factor f is typically
much lower than that of the observed vector y. Nevertheless, we see merit in each approach, and which, if
either, is superior is ultimately an empirical matter in
specific applications. Perhaps one could also allow for
stochastic volatility in *both* the measurement and transition shocks, although one would have to confront the
resulting identification issues.

Interestingly, much of both the "transition shock
stochastic volatility" work (Hautsch and Ou (2008),
Hautsch and Yang (2010)) and "measurement shock
stochastic volatility" work (Laurini and Hotta (2010))
discussed above proceeds in Bayesian fashion, using
Markov-chain Monte Carlo as a powerful computational

device to facilitate estimation and inference in complex models that include time-varying parameters and stochastic volatility. Introduction of informative priors would be a natural next step, allowing for shrinkage with potential benefits to forecasting.

4.3.2 AFNS Formulation

Thus far we have focused on stochastic volatility in DNS environments, but it can also be incorporated in the AFNS environment.

Modern arbitrage-free yield curve modeling started with the one-factor model of Vasicek (1977), as extended to the multifactor case by Langetieg (1980). Such models were significantly clarified and extended by Duffie and Kan (1996), Dai and Singleton (2000), Duffee (2002), and Joslin et al. (2011b).

In the canonical $A_m(N)$ representation of Dai and Singleton (2000) (N yield factors driving m square-root volatility processes), fixed volatility corresponds to $m = 0$. Such models are also known as "Gaussian" because the Brownian shocks that drive them produce Gaussian distributions in the absence of stochastic volatility.[17]

Gaussian models remain popular in theory, as they seem to achieve reasonable descriptive accuracy while maintaining analytic tractability, whereas stochastic volatility in arbitrage-free models is widely believed to present significant mathematical challenges. Nevertheless, as an empirical matter, stochastic volatility is clearly present in bond yield data.[18]

---

[17] By "stochastic volatility" we mean to include a variety of possible patterns of dynamic conditional heteroskedasticity, including observation-driven processes as in the GARCH family and parameter-driven processes as in the (so-called, confusingly) stochastic volatility family. See section 3.2 of Andersen et al. (2010).

[18] See, for example, Andersen et al. (2006).

Against this background, Christensen et al. (2010a) incorporate stochastic volatility into the risk-neutral yield factor dynamics in otherwise standard AFNS models. They show that, despite the introduction of stochastic volatility, the yield-adjustment term remains constant in each case, depending only on maturity and not on time. They show moreover that five varieties of $A_m(3)$ are possible while still respecting AFNS structure: two $A_1(3)$ AFNS models with stochastic volatility entering through the level or curvature factor; two $A_2(3)$ AFNS models with stochastic volatility entering through the level and curvature or slope and curvature factors; and an $A_3(3)$ AFNS model with stochastic volatility entering through all three factors.

The Christensen et al. (2010a) empirical results indicate that the yield level factor is the most important driver of stochastic volatility, but that the slope and curvature factors also contribute to volatility dynamics. Hence the richest model considered, $A_3(3)$ AFNS, is also the relatively most successful.

4.3.3   Spanned and Unspanned Volatility

Although $A_3(3)$ AFNS is most successful in relative terms, Christensen et al. (2010a) show that it nevertheless performs poorly in absolute terms.[19] It fails to match realized volatility, even as a rough approximation. Indeed the correlation between fitted $A_3(3)$ AFNS stochastic volatility and realized volatility is low over long periods, and *negative* during the post-1991 period.

This apparent inability of the factors that span bond yields simultaneously to span yield volatility has been

---

[19] This result echoes Dai and Singleton (2002), who also argue that $A_3(3)$ models are too restrictive to capture stochastic volatility.

noticed by several authors in various arbitrage-free environments, including Collin-Dufresne et al. (2008), Jacobs and Karoui (2009), and Andersen and Benzoni (2010). Such "unspanned stochastic volatility" is often viewed as a puzzle, but at some level it seems unlikely that the factors that drive the conditional means of yields should *necessarily* also drive their conditional variances.[20] In any event, our understanding of the factors driving yield volatility clearly remains poor despite several recent and sophisticated attempts. The situation is reminiscent of much of the financial asset return volatility modeling literature, which although often successful at reduced-form modeling and forecasting, nevertheless is silent regarding the fundamental determinants of volatility.[21]

4.4 Macroeconomic Fundamentals

Perhaps surprisingly given its natural links to the macroeconomy, thus far we have approached the yield curve from an almost exclusively finance viewpoint. Here we begin to broaden the discussion to include links to macroeconomic fundamentals, focusing mostly on DNS-style modeling that correlates aspects of the yield curve with aspects of the macroeconomy, paving the way for the macro-finance economic analyses of the next chapter.

One could proceed from a unidirectional perspective, for example, using the yield curve to explain or forecast macroeconomic variables. In a DNS environment, the "yield curve" is simply L_t, S_t, and C_t, so that one can effectively "regress variables on the yield curve" by regressing on L_t, S_t, and C_t. For example, Nyholm (2007)

---

[20] Alternatively, perhaps models with more than three factors would be more successful in capturing stochastic volatility.

[21] See Diebold and Yilmaz (2010).

uses the entire yield curve, as distilled into level, slope, and curvature factors, to forecast recessions, thereby generalizing earlier work such as Estrella and Mishkin (1998) that forecasts real activity exclusively via the yield curve slope.[22]

Although interesting and important, results based on the unidirectional perspective are surely lacking, insofar as richer dynamic interactions among yield factors and macroeconomic fundamentals are operative. In particular, those dynamic interactions likely involve bidirectional causality, or "feedback." We will briefly sketch both two-step and one-step modeling approaches that allow incorporation and assessment of such effects.

4.4.1   Two-Step DNS Approaches

In the two-step DNS approach to yield modeling and forecasting, we first extract time series of yield factors (step 1) and then fit a dynamic model such as a vector autoregression to those extracted factors (step 2). One can immediately allow for interactions among yield factors and macroeconomic fundamentals by augmenting the second-step vector autoregression with candidate macroeconomic variables reflecting inflation, real activity, and so forth.[23] We focus on single-country models, but the same framework relates to multicountry models.[24]

Instead of linking yield factors to each of a small set of macroeconomic variables, one could alternatively link yield factors to macroeconomic *factors* extracted from a

---

[22] See also Bianchi et al. (2009) and Chauvet and Senyuz (2009).

[23] Work in that tradition includes Cassola and Porter (2011) and Hoffmaister et al. (2010).

[24] For example, Tam and Yu (2008) extend Diebold et al. (2008) to include macroeconomic fundamentals.

large set of macroeconomic variables. In such a "big-data" (Diebold (2003)) or "data-rich" (Bernanke and Boivin (2003)) or "factor-augmented" (Bernanke et al. (2005)) two-step procedure, one first extracts yield factors (level, slope, curvature) and macroeconomic factors (e.g., broad nominal activity and broad real activity), and then analyzes all factors in a joint vector autoregression.[25] Indeed, De Pooter et al. (2010) argue that macroeconomic variables interact best with the yield curve when introduced as factors from data-rich environments.[26]

It is worth noting that one could also link yield curve factors to macroeconomic factors at very high frequency. The yield curve is of course available at high frequency (e.g., daily), but high-frequency "nowcasts" of real activity are now available as well, as in Aruoba et al. (2009), Aruoba and Diebold (2010), and Aruoba et al. (2011).

4.4.2 One-Step DNS Approaches

The one-step approach uses a state-space framework, but with the state vector expanded to include macroeconomic variables, as in Diebold et al. (2006b) and Joslin et al. (2009).[27] This produces the modified transition and measurement equations

$$(f_t - \mu) = A(f_{t-1} - \mu) + \eta_t,$$
$$y_t = \Lambda f_t + \varepsilon_t,$$
$$\begin{pmatrix} \eta_t \\ \varepsilon_t \end{pmatrix} \sim WN \left(\begin{pmatrix} 0 \\ 0 \end{pmatrix}, \begin{pmatrix} Q & 0 \\ 0 & H \end{pmatrix} \right),$$

---

[25] Macroeconomic factors are commonly extracted in data-rich environments as the first few principal components, as in Stock and Watson (1999).

[26] See also Mönch (2008) and Favero et al. (2011).

[27] Related earlier work includes Carriero et al. (2006).

where $f_t' = (L_t, S_t, C_t, X_t)$, X_t is a vector of macro-economic fundamentals, and the dimensions of A, μ, η_t, and Q are increased as appropriate.[28]

Diebold et al. (2006b), for example, use an X consisting of inflation, capacity utilization, and the federal funds rate.[29] They find strong evidence of bidirectional causality from yield factors to macroeconomic variables and from macroeconomic variables to yield factors. Moreover, they find that the stronger causal direction is from the macroeconomy to the yield curve. Overall, the evidence on strength of causal direction appears mixed, with other authors (e.g., Favero et al. (2011)) emphasizing the yields-to-macro direction. The ultimate point, of course, is that there is no need to attempt to declare one or the other causal direction stronger; both can be important.

One could also move to a data-rich one-step framework. A first and simple approach would be to replace the small number of individual macroeconomic indicators in X with a similarly small number of macroeconomic *factors* obtained from a much larger set of indicators.

Of course this data-rich one-step estimator isn't *truly* one-step, as it is based on separately extracted macroeconomic factors. In principle, one could produce a true one-step analysis by including in the observed vector y not only the set of observed bond yields but also the full set of (potentially many dozens of) macroeconomic indicators. Traditional iterative numerical maximum-likelihood estimation of such a system

---

[28] In particular, Λ is now $N \times (3 + K)$, but the K rightmost columns contain only zeros so that the yields still load only on the yield curve factors. This form is consistent with the view that only three factors are needed to distill the information in the yield curve.

[29] We shall discuss aspects of this choice of macroeconomic variables shortly.

would be infeasible, but the methods of Jungbacker and Koopman (2008) may render it tractable.

4.4.3 The Macroeconomy and Yield Factors

Much work has focused on the links of yield level, slope, and curvature factors to macroeconomic fundamentals. Although surely it is not possible to label various macroeconomic fundamentals as uniquely linked to level, or slope, or curvature, some important relationships need to be discussed.

First, consider level. Economic theory broadly suggests that the nominal yield curve level should be linked to the level of expected inflation. Koopman et al. (2010b), for example, argue that long-run inflation expectations drive the level factor, in the tradition of the Kozicki and Tinsley (2001) "shifting endpoints" model. Expected inflation is of course often linked to current actual inflation. In any event, some measure related to inflation is the obvious macroeconomic fundamental associated with the level factor.[30] Hence the inclusion of inflation as a macroeconomic fundamental in Diebold et al. (2006b).

Second, consider slope. A similarly broad interpretation of economic theory suggests that yield curve slope should be linked to real activity, although the stories and causal directions of the relationship can differ. One channel is from yields to real activity. For example, when central banks tighten monetary policy, the short rate increases, and a recession often follows. Hence inverted yield curves may tend to precede recessions. Another

---

[30] It is interesting to note that the level factor is a unit-root process under the Q-measure and is generally found to be highly persistent under the P-measure, as is inflation.

channel is from expected future real activity to yields. Good news about near-term productivity, for example, will tend to raise shorter-term rates, suggesting that inverted yield curves precede *booms.*

Estrella and Mishkin (1998) and Stock and Watson (2003) provide evidence favoring the "policy channel," and Kurmann and Otrok (2010) provide evidence favoring the "good news channel." The policy and supply shock effects may partially offset each other, but in any event, variables related to current or expected future real activity are obvious slope fundamentals. Hence capacity utilization is included as a macroeconomic fundamental in Diebold et al. (2006b).

Third, consider curvature—a less important but somewhat difficult to interpret factor. Via a convexity argument, one might conjecture a link between the curvature factor and the volatility of the level factor.[31] Indeed Litterman et al. (1991) take precisely that route and obtain good empirical results. To the best of our knowledge, however, their results are difficult to replicate on more recent and non-U.S. data.[32]

Simultaneously, and perhaps fortunately, curvature is responsible for relatively little yield curve variation. As typically happens with economic and financial data, a single factor explains most of yield variation, and a second factor explains much of the rest, leaving only a very small role for a third. In a sense, this makes our lack of understanding of curvature less unfortunate than it otherwise would be.

The role of curvature is relatively minor not only under the *P*-measure but also under the AFNS *Q*-measure. Recall the risk-neutral AFNS dynamics stated

---

[31] For a good exposition of bond convexity, see Neftci (2004).

[32] We have tried, with mixed success at best.

earlier in equation (3.12), which we reproduce here for convenience:

$$
\begin{pmatrix} dX_t^1 \\ dX_t^2 \\ dX_t^3 \end{pmatrix} = \begin{pmatrix} 0 & 0 & 0 \\ 0 & \lambda & -\lambda \\ 0 & 0 & \lambda \end{pmatrix} \left[\begin{pmatrix} \theta_1^Q \\ \theta_2^Q \\ \theta_3^Q \end{pmatrix} - \begin{pmatrix} X_t^1 \\ X_t^2 \\ X_t^3 \end{pmatrix} \right] dt
$$

$$
+ \begin{pmatrix} \sigma_{11} & \sigma_{12} & \sigma_{13} \\ \sigma_{21} & \sigma_{22} & \sigma_{23} \\ \sigma_{31} & \sigma_{32} & \sigma_{33} \end{pmatrix} \begin{pmatrix} dW_t^{1,Q} \\ dW_t^{2,Q} \\ dW_t^{3,Q} \end{pmatrix}, \quad \lambda > 0.
$$

Note in particular that under the Q-measure nothing Granger-causes curvature, and curvature Granger-causes only the slope factor.

Because of curvature's limited role in both the P- and Q-measures, and because of the limited understanding of its relation to the macroeconomy, when augmenting the DNS state vector Diebold et al. (2006b) do not include a macroeconomic fundamental conjectured to drive curvature.

Finally, consider the role of policy. If central banks control the short rate, and if medium and long rates are linked to expected future short rates, then the entire yield curve (level, slope, curvature) should be linked to current and expected future policy. It is interesting to note that, unlike the macroeconomic fundamentals discussed thus far, which are linked to specific yield factors, macroeconomic policy may potentially affect *all* yield factors, depending on bond market perceptions and expectations of policy. In part for this reason, Diebold et al. (2006b) include a policy variable, the federal funds rate, in their analysis of bond yields and macroeconomic fundamentals.

4.4.4   On Nominal vs. Real Yields

In closing this chapter, we wish to emphasize certain aspects of the distinction between nominal and real yields from a DNS/AFNS perspective.

We follow the finance literature throughout this book in our emphasis on nominal yields. Nominal yields are based on observed prices of traded instruments, while the construction of real yields often requires additional assumptions about inflation expectations formation and inflation risk tolerance (the latter by typically invoking Fisherian risk neutrality). Notwithstanding possible difficulties associated with calculating real yields, they are obviously important from certain perspectives—particularly macroeconomic perspectives—and it is worth considering them in the DNS/AFNS context. Several remarks are in order.

First, in a crude sense, DNS/AFNS modeling of nominal yield curves may be able to capture movements in real yields. Suppose movements in expected inflation affect nominal yields only through the nominal yield curve level factor. Then, keeping the level factor fixed at its average value, say, the movements in the nominal yield curve coming from the remaining time-varying slope and curvature factors are indicative of movements in the real yield curve.

Second, if real yields or some approximation to them are available, then DNS or AFNS can be used to model them. For example, one could simply declare the "real yield" approximations of interest to be nominal yields less break-even inflation extracted from indexed bonds, and model them using DNS.[33] Alternatively, one could model ex-post as opposed to ex-ante real yields.

---

[33] Indexed bonds have been available for some time in many countries, including the United States.

Finally, AFNS could be used with indexed bond yields in a much more sophisticated way to extract real yields without invoking risk neutrality; that is, allowing for inflation risk premia. In Chapter 5, we discuss this in detail, along with several other macro-finance topics, to which we now turn.

5

Macro-Finance

From the vantage point of incorporating macroeconomic considerations into yield curve modeling, one can view the approaches introduced previously in section 4.4 as preparatory, paving the way for more extensive explorations. In this chapter, we move in that direction, discussing a variety of AFNS macro-finance yield curve approaches.

5.1   Macro-Finance Yield Curve Modeling

A key feature of the recent global financial crisis and recession is the close feedback between the real economy and financial conditions. In many countries, the credit and asset price boom that preceded the crisis coincided with strong spending and production. Similarly, during the crash, deteriorating financial conditions both contributed to the deep declines in economic activity and were exacerbated by them. Still, modeling this close feedback poses a significant challenge to macroeconomists and finance economists because of the long-standing separation between the two disciplines. In macro models, the entire financial sector is often represented by a single interest rate with no accounting for credit or liquidity risk and no role for financial intermediation or financial frictions. Similarly, finance models often focus on the consistency of asset prices across markets with little regard for underlying macroeconomic fundamentals. To understand important aspects of the recent financial crisis and, more generally, the intertwined dynamics of interest rates and the economy, a joint macro-finance perspective is likely necessary.

Of course, differences between the finance and macro perspectives reflect in part different questions of interest and different avenues for exploration; however, it is striking that there is so little interchange or overlap between the two research literatures. At the very least, it suggests that there may be synergies from combining elements of each. From a finance perspective, the short rate is a fundamental building block for rates of other maturities, because long yields are driven in significant part by expected future short rates. From a macro perspective, the short rate is a key monetary policy instrument, which is adjusted by the central bank to achieve economic stabilization goals. Taken together, a joint macro-finance perspective would suggest that understanding the central bank policy response to fundamental macroeconomic shocks should explain movements in the short end of the yield curve; furthermore, with the consistency between long and short rates enforced by the no-arbitrage assumption, expected future macroeconomic variation should account for movements farther out in the yield curve as well.

One key strand of macro-finance research examines the finance implications for bond pricing in a model with macroeconomic variables. As a theoretical matter, the term premium on a long-term nominal bond compensates investors for inflation and consumption risks over

the lifetime of the bond.[1] A large finance literature finds
that these risk premiums are substantial and vary significantly over time, as, for example, in Campbell and
Shiller (1991) and Cochrane and Piazzesi (2005). However, Backus et al. (1989) find the standard consumption-
based asset pricing model of an endowment economy cannot account for such large and variable term premiums.
The basic inability of a standard macro-finance model to
generate a sufficiently large and variable nominal bond
risk premium has been termed the "bond premium puzzle." More recently, Wachter (2006), Piazzesi and Schneider (2006), and Bansal and Shaliastovich (2010) have
had some success in resolving the bond premium puzzle within an endowment economy by using preferences
that have been modified to include either an important
role for habit, as in Campbell and Cochrane (1999), or
"recursive utility," as in Epstein and Zin (1989).

The progress in resolving the bond premium puzzle in
an endowment economy remains somewhat unsatisfying
from a macro perspective because the lack of a complete set of macroeconomic structural relationships pre-
cludes studying some important questions. Accordingly,
interest in extending the endowment economy results to
more fully specified dynamic stochastic general equilibrium (DSGE) models has been growing.[2] Unfortunately,
Rudebusch and Swanson (2008) find that a standard
DSGE model cannot replicate the size and variability of
the bond premium in the data. However, by augmenting

---

[1] Even a default-free nominal bond is risky if its price covaries
with the bondholder's marginal utility of consumption. If times
of high inflation are correlated with times of low output, then a
nominal bond loses value just when the investor values consumption
the most, so it would carry a risk premium.

[2] See, for example, Bekaert et al. (2010), Hördahl et al. (2008),
and Gallmeyer et al. (2005).

the standard DSGE model with Epstein-Zin preferences, Rudebusch and Swanson (2012) have had greater success in matching both basic macroeconomic moments (e.g., the standard deviations of consumption and inflation) and basic bond pricing moments (e.g., the means and volatilities of the yield curve slope and bond excess holding period returns). Still, although Epstein-Zin preferences appear useful in letting the DSGE model replicate certain bond pricing facts without compromising its ability to fit macroeconomic facts, the DSGE model financial sector remains far too rudimentary in terms of financial frictions and intermediation.[3]

A second strand of macro-finance research adds macro, in the form of macroeconomic variables or theoretical structure, to the canonical finance affine arbitrage-free term structure model. As described earlier, the usual finance model decomposes the short-term interest rate into unobserved factors that are modeled as autoregressive time series that are unrelated to macroeconomic variation. In contrast, from a macro perspective, the short rate is determined by macroeconomic variables in the context of a monetary policy reaction function. The Rudebusch and Wu (2008) model reconciles these two views in a macro-finance framework that has term structure factors jointly estimated with macroeconomic relationships. In particular, this model combines an affine

---

[3] Interesting new DSGE work, however, progresses significantly. A leading example is van Binsbergen et al. (2010), who emphasize the endogeneity of both capital and labor in a fully articulated production economy. In such environments, bond yields must satisfy a no-arbitrage condition involving the user cost of capital, which puts challenging restrictions on admissible investment, capital and asset-price dynamics. The upshot is that, even if empirically accurate macro-yields interaction in fully specified DSGE models remains elusive, we now have much greater understanding of the reasons.

arbitrage-free term structure model with a small New Keynesian rational expectations macroeconomic model with the short-term interest rate related to macroeconomic fundamentals through a monetary policy reaction function. This combined framework is able to interpret the latent factors of the yield curve in terms of macroeconomic variables, with the level factor identified as a perceived inflation target and the slope factor identified as a cyclical monetary policy response to the economy.[4]

Two applications of the Rudebusch-Wu model illustrate the range of issues that such a macro-finance model can address. First, Rudebusch and Wu (2007) use this model to consider whether the bond market's assessment of risk has shifted in such a way as to shed light on the Great Moderation—the period of reduced macroeconomic volatility from around 1985 to 2007. Indeed, they find that the volatility of term premiums over time reflects declines in the conditional volatility and price of risk attached to the level factor, which is linked in the model to investors' perceptions of the central bank's inflation target. The payoff from a macro-finance analysis is thus bidirectional. The macro contribution illuminates the nature of the shift in the behavior of the term structure, highlighting the importance of a shift in investors' views regarding the risk associated with the inflation goals of the monetary authority. The finance contribution suggests that more than just good luck was responsible for the subdued macroeconomic outcomes. Instead, a favorable change in economic dynamics, likely linked to a shift in the monetary policy environment, may have been an important element of the Great Moderation.

---

[4] Related research includes Ang and Piazzesi (2003), Dewachter and Lyrio (2006, 2008), Wright (2011), Joslin et al. (2009), De Pooter et al. (2010), and Hördahl et al. (2006).

As a second application of the Rudebusch-Wu model, Rudebusch et al. (2006) examine the so-called conundrum of surprisingly low long-term bond yields from 2004 to 2006. They find that during this episode, nominal 10-year yields are unusually low—on the order of 40 to 50 basis points. However, despite examining several popular explanations for the conundrum by regressing the model's residuals on various proxies for uncertainty or volatility, the unusually low levels of long-term interest rates remained mostly unaccounted for. Of course, with the benefit of hindsight, the bond yield conundrum now appears to have been part of a broader global credit boom that was characterized by an underpricing of many types of risk, especially for fixed-income securities. Uncovering the source of that credit boom—the antecedent for the subsequent credit bust and financial crisis—remains an important area of future research, and a macro-finance perspective is likely to be useful in that investigation.

5.2   Macro-Finance and AFNS

The combination of macro and finance can also be accomplished with the AFNS model. Indeed, the AFNS factor structure provides a very useful framework for examining various macro-finance questions given the computational difficulties in extending finance-only affine arbitrage-free models.

5.2.1   Inflation Expectations and Risk

One application of the AFNS model, in Christensen et al. (2010c), produces estimates of the inflation expectations of financial market participants from prices of nominal and real bonds. While nominal bonds have a fixed

notional principal, real bonds are directly indexed to
overall price inflation. For example, the principal and
coupon payments of U.S. Treasury inflation-protected
securities (TIPS) vary with the consumer price index.
Differences between comparable-maturity nominal and
real yields are known as break-even inflation (BEI) rates.
However, BEI rates are imperfect measures of inflation
expectations because they also include compensation for
inflation risk. That is, a BEI rate could rise if future
inflation uncertainty rose or if investors required greater
compensation for that uncertainty, even if expectations
for the future level of inflation remained unchanged.
Obtaining a timely decomposition of BEI rates into inflation expectations and inflation risk premiums is of keen
interest to market participants, researchers, and central
bankers.

The decomposition of a BEI rate into inflation expectations and an inflation risk premium depends on the correlations between inflation and the unobserved stochastic discount factors of investors. Such a decomposition
requires a model, and Christensen et al. (2010c) use an
affine four-factor AFNS model for this purpose. This
model links yield curve dynamics and investor risk premiums within a consistent framework that can produce
both risk-neutral and real-world representations of yield
curves over time. Denote the nominal and real stochastic discount factors as M_t^N and M_t^R, respectively. The
price of a nominal bond that pays one dollar at time τ
and the price of a real bond that pays one unit of the
consumption basket at time τ are written as

$$P_t^N(\tau) = E_t^P \left[\frac{M_{t+\tau}^N}{M_t^N} \right] \quad \text{and} \quad P_t^R(\tau) = E_t^P \left[\frac{M_{t+\tau}^R}{M_t^R} \right].$$

The no-arbitrage condition requires a consistency between the prices of nominal and real bonds such that

the price of the consumption basket, denoted as the overall price level Q_t, is the ratio of the stochastic discount factors:

$$Q_t = \frac{M_t^R}{M_t^N}.$$

The relationship between nominal and real zero-coupon yields with maturity τ at time t, denoted as $y_t^N(\tau)$ and $y_t^R(\tau)$, and expected inflation can be derived as

$$y_t^N(\tau) = y_t^R(\tau) + \pi_t^e(\tau) + \phi_t(\tau),$$

where the market-implied rate of inflation expected at time t for the period from t to $t + \tau$ is

$$\pi_t^e(\tau) = -\frac{1}{\tau} \ln E_t^P \left[\frac{Q_t}{Q_{t+\tau}} \right]$$

$$= -\frac{1}{\tau} \ln E_t^P \left[\exp \left(-\int_t^{t+\tau} (r_s^N - r_s^R) ds \right) \right],$$

and r_t^N and r_t^R are the instantaneous nominal and real risk-free rates. The corresponding inflation risk premium is denoted as

$$\phi_t(\tau) = -\frac{1}{\tau} \ln \left(1 + \frac{\text{cov}_t^P [M_{t+\tau}^R / M_t^R, Q_t/Q_{t+\tau}]}{E_t^P [M_{t+\tau}^R / M_t^R] \times E_t^P [Q_t/Q_{t+\tau}]} \right).$$

Nominal and real yields are then modeled with a four-factor AFNS representation. The first three factors correspond to the level, slope, and curvature factors commonly observed for nominal yields and denoted L_t^N, S_t, and C_t, respectively. The fourth factor, L_t^R, corresponds to the level factor for real yields. The state vector is thus defined as $X_t = (L_t^N, S_t, C_t, L_t^R)$. The instantaneous nominal and real risk-free rates are set to be

$$r_t^N = L_t^N + S_t \quad \text{and} \quad r_t^R = L_t^R + \alpha^R S_t,$$

where the differential scaling of real rates to the common slope factor is captured by the parameter α^R. Within this framework, nominal Treasury zero-coupon bond yields are denoted as

$$
y_t^N(\tau) = L_t^N + \left(\frac{1 - e^{-\lambda\tau}}{\lambda\tau}\right) S_t
$$
$$
+ \left(\frac{1 - e^{-\lambda\tau}}{\lambda\tau} - e^{-\lambda\tau}\right) C_t + \frac{A^N(\tau)}{\tau},
$$

where $A^N(\tau)/\tau$ is a nominal yield-adjustment term. The real TIPS zero-coupon bond yields are

$$
y_t^R(\tau) = L_t^R + \alpha^R \left(\frac{1 - e^{-\lambda\tau}}{\lambda\tau}\right) S_t
$$
$$
+ \alpha^R \left(\frac{1 - e^{-\lambda\tau}}{\lambda\tau} - e^{-\lambda\tau}\right) C_t + \frac{A^R(\tau)}{\tau},
$$

where $A^R(\tau)/\tau$ is a real yield-adjustment term. These two equations when combined in state-space form constitute the measurement equation within a Kalman filter estimation.

The complete model also requires specifying the price of risk, which determines the connection between the risk-neutral and real-world yield dynamics. The nominal and real stochastic discount factors are given standard dynamics $dM_t^N/M_t^N = -r_t^N dt - \Gamma_t'^{P} t$ and $dM_t^R/M_t^R = -r_t^R dt - \Gamma_t'^{P} t$. With essentially affine risk premium specification introduced by Duffee (2002), the risk premium Γ_t is defined by the measure change

$$
dW_t^Q = dW_t^P + \Gamma_t dt,
$$

with $\Gamma_t = \gamma^0 + \gamma^1 X_t$, $\gamma^0 \in \mathbf{R}^4$, and $\gamma^1 \in \mathbf{R}^{4\times 4}$, where W_t^P is a Brownian motion process. Therefore, the real-world dynamics of the state variables can be expressed as

$$dX_t = K^P(\theta^P - X_t)dt + \Sigma dW_t^P.$$

In the unrestricted case, both K^P and θ^P are allowed to vary freely, but Christensen et al. (2010c) provide a detailed empirical analysis to justify various zero-value restrictions on the K^P matrix. Their estimation uses nominal Treasury zero-coupon bond yields with maturities of 3 and 6 months, and 1, 2, 3, 5, 7, and 10 years and real TIPS bond yields with maturities of 5, 6, 7, 8, 9, and 10 years.[5]

The joint four-factor arbitrage-free model fits both the nominal and real yield curves quite well. Figure 5.1 shows the 5- and 10-year nominal and real zero-coupon yields and their differences—that is, the associated observed BEI rates, which have changed little on balance since 2004. Figure 5.1 also compares these observed BEI rates to comparable-maturity model-implied BEI rates, which are calculated as the differences between the fitted nominal and real yields from the estimated joint AFNS model. The small differences between the observed and model-implied BEI rates reflect the overall good fit of the model.

This joint AFNS model also can decompose the BEI rate into inflation expectations and the inflation risk premia at various horizons. Given the estimated model parameters and the estimated paths of the four state variables, the model-implied average 5- and 10-year expected inflation series are illustrated in Figure 5.2. The

---

[5] The U.S. Treasury first issued TIPS in 1997, but for several years afterward the liquidity of the secondary TIPS market was impaired by the small amount of securities outstanding and uncertainty about the Treasury's commitment to the program. To avoid the illiquid nascent years of this market, the estimation sample of TIPS yields starts in 2003.

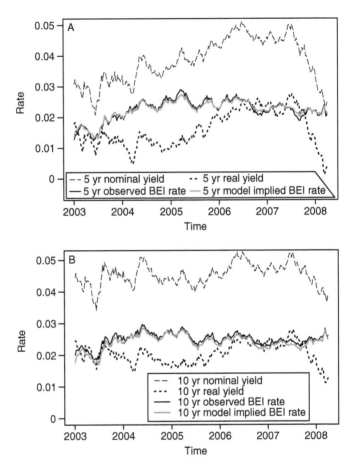

Figure 5.1. Nominal and Real Yields and BEI Rates. We plot nominal and real zero-coupon U.S. Treasury yields with associated break-even inflation (BEI) rates and implied BEI rates from the joint AFNS model. A: Five-year maturity. B: Ten-year maturity.

model's estimates of inflation expectations were generated using only nominal and real yields without any data on inflation or inflation expectations. To provide some

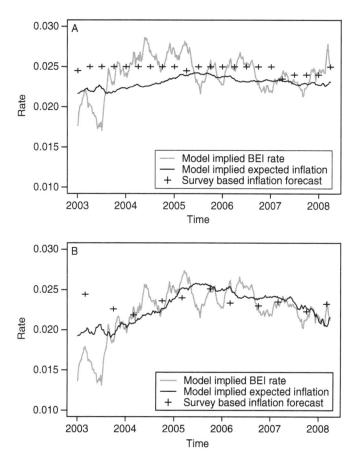

Figure 5.2. BEI Rates and Expected Inflation. We plot break-even inflation (BEI) rates, average expected inflation rates implied from the joint AFNS model, and survey-based measures of inflation expectations. A: Five-year maturity. B: Ten-year maturity.

independent indication of accuracy, Figure 5.2 also plots survey-based measures of expectations of CPI inflation, which are obtained from the Blue Chip Consensus survey

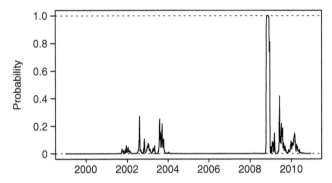

Figure 5.3.   Probabilities of Nonpositive Net Inflation. We show the probability of nonpositive net inflation (or deflation) over the forthcoming year as estimated over the full sample period.

at the 5-year horizon and from the Survey of Professional Forecasters at the 10-year horizon. The relatively close match between the model-implied and the survey-based measures of inflation expectations provides further support for the model's decomposition of the BEI rate.

Besides point forecasts, this model can also be used to calculate the entire probability distribution of future inflation outcomes. For example, in recent years, as inflation rates around the world have fallen to much lower levels, the risk of negative inflation—price deflation— has become a recurring concern for several central banks.[6] Christensen et al. (2011b) use the above model to construct probability forecasts for episodes of price

---

[6] If deflations are special regimes that have their own unique dynamics or social costs, it would be particularly useful to go beyond point forecasts of inflation and consider probability forecasts for the occurrence of a deflationary episode. Similar arguments have long been used to motivate the widespread focus on recession probability forecasts (e.g., Diebold and Rudebusch (1989)).

deflation. Figure 5.3 shows the resulting estimates of the one-year probability of deflation. The estimated deflation probability is typically zero, except for two notable deflation scare episodes. The first episode followed the 2001 recession. During this period, Federal Reserve policymakers expressed concern for the first time that inflation might fall too low. The second deflation scare episode began shortly after the Lehman Brothers bankruptcy on September 15, 2008, and ran through April 2010. This episode is marked by a sharp spike in the fitted, one-year deflation probabilities in late October and early November 2008.[7] In response to concerns of a very severe and rapid economic collapse, the Federal Reserve enacted a variety of conventional and unconventional monetary and liquidity policy actions, which likely helped reduce the probabilities in the first quarter of 2009.

5.2.2 Liquidity and Interbank Lending Rates

A second macro-finance application of the AFNS model, provided in Christensen et al. (2009), investigates the effect of the new central bank liquidity facilities that were instituted during the financial crisis. In early August 2007, amid declining prices and credit ratings for U.S. mortgage-backed securities and other forms of structured credit, international money markets came under severe stress. Short-term funding rates in the interbank market rose sharply relative to yields on comparable-maturity

---

[7] The very high deflation probabilities immediately after the Lehman bankruptcy reflect widespread fears of a global macroeconomic catastrophe, but they are also likely boosted by market illiquidity during the financial crisis. However, the impaired liquidity appears to have lasted only a few months.

government securities. For example, the three-month U.S. dollar London interbank offered rate (LIBOR) jumped from only 20 basis points higher than the three-month U.S. Treasury yield during the first seven months of 2007 to over 110 basis points higher during the final five months of the year. This enlarged spread was also remarkable for persisting into 2009.

LIBOR rates are widely used as reference rates in financial instruments, including derivatives contracts, variable-rate home mortgages, and corporate notes, so their unusually high levels appeared likely to have widespread adverse financial and macroeconomic repercussions. To limit these adverse effects, central banks around the world established an extraordinary set of lending facilities that were intended to increase financial market liquidity and ease strains in term interbank funding markets, especially at maturities of a few months or more. Specifically, on December 12, 2007, the Bank of Canada, the Bank of England, the European Central Bank (ECB), the Federal Reserve, and the Swiss National Bank jointly announced a set of measures designed to address elevated pressures in term funding markets. The Federal Reserve also announced a new Term Auction Facility, or TAF, to provide depository institutions with a source of term funding.

Christensen et al. (2009) assess the effect of the establishment of these extraordinary central bank liquidity facilities on the interbank lending market and, in particular, on term LIBOR spreads over Treasury yields. In theory, the provision of central bank liquidity could lower the liquidity premium on interbank debt through a variety of channels. On the supply side, banks that have a greater assurance of meeting their own unforeseen liquidity needs over time should be more willing to extend term loans to other banks. In addition, creditors should be more willing to provide funding to banks that have easy and dependable access to funds, since there is a greater reassurance of timely repayment. On the demand side, with a central bank liquidity backstop, banks should be less inclined to borrow from other banks to satisfy any precautionary demand for liquid funds because their future idiosyncratic demands for liquidity over time can be met via the backstop. However, assessing the relative importance of these channels is difficult. Furthermore, judging the efficacy of central bank liquidity facilities in lowering the liquidity premium is complicated because LIBOR rates, which are for unsecured bank deposits, also include a credit risk premium for the possibility that the borrowing bank may default. The elevated LIBOR spreads during the financial crisis likely reflected both higher credit risk and liquidity premiums, so any assessment of the effect of the recent extraordinary central bank liquidity provisions must also control for fluctuations in bank credit risk.

To analyze the effectiveness of the central bank liquidity facilities in reducing interbank lending pressures, Christensen et al. (2009) estimate an affine arbitrage-free term structure representation of U.S. Treasury yields, the yields on bonds issued by financial institutions, and term LIBOR rates using weekly data from 1995 to midyear 2008. The resulting six-factor AFNS representation provides arbitrage-free joint pricing of Treasury yields, financial corporate bond yields, and LIBOR rates. Three factors account for Treasury yields, two factors capture bank debt risk dynamics, and a third factor is specific to LIBOR rates. This structure can decompose movements in LIBOR rates into changes in bank debt risk premiums and changes in a factor specific to the interbank market that includes a liquidity premium. It also allows hypothesis testing and counterfactual analysis related to the introduction of the central bank liquidity facilities.

The model results support the view that the central bank liquidity facilities established in December 2007 helped lower LIBOR rates. Specifically, the parameters governing the term LIBOR factor within the model change after the introduction of the liquidity facilities. The hypothesis of constant parameters is overwhelmingly rejected, suggesting that the behavior of this factor, and thus of the LIBOR market, was directly affected by the introduction of central bank liquidity facilities. To quantify the impact that the introduction of the liquidity facilities had on the interbank market, Christensen et al. (2009) conduct a counterfactual analysis of what would have happened had they *not* been introduced. The full-sample model—without the regime switch—generates the actual and counterfactual paths for the three-month LIBOR rate. The latter suggests what that spread *might* have been if it had been priced in accordance with prevailing conditions in the Treasury and corporate bond markets for U.S. financial firms.

Figure 5.4 illustrates the effect of the counterfactual path on the three-month LIBOR spread over the three-month Treasuries since the beginning of 2007. Note that the model-implied three-month LIBOR spread is close to the observed spread over this period. From the start of the financial crisis—which was triggered by an August 9, 2007, announcement by the French bank BNP Paribas—until the TAF and joint central bank swap announcement in mid-December 2007, the observed LIBOR rate averaged 8 basis points higher than the counterfactual rate. However, by the end of 2007, a significant wedge

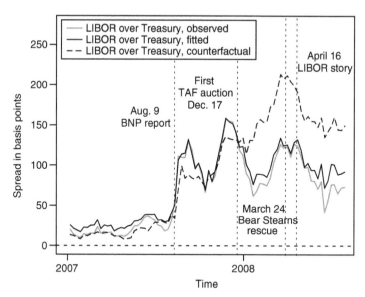

Figure 5.4. LIBOR Spreads. We show observed and fitted three-month LIBOR rate spreads over the three-month Treasuries in a six-factor model and a counterfactual model-based spread when the LIBOR-specific factor is fixed at its historical average prior to December 14, 2007.

developed between the two. As of the end of the sample on July 25, 2008, the difference between the counterfactual spread and the observed three-month LIBOR spread was 82 basis points. Therefore, this analysis suggests that the three-month LIBOR rate would have been *higher* in the absence of the central bank liquidity facilities. Accordingly, the announcement of the central bank liquidity facilities on December 12, 2007, likely affected the interbank lending market in the intended way; that is, the increased provision of bank liquidity by central banks lowered LIBOR rates relative to where they might have been in the absence of these actions.

5.3   Evolving Research Directions

The macro-finance term structure literature is in its infancy, with many important questions yet to answer. The importance of this research has only been heightened by the latest financial turmoil and economic recession. These recent events were triggered in part by a "fixed-income crisis" involving nominal bonds of various maturities and risk characteristics, which suggests that a better macro-finance understanding of bond pricing and risk premiums may be helpful in elucidating them. However, much of the research surveyed here predates the latest crisis episode and can form only part of a foundation for a broader research agenda to develop a better understanding of the relevant macro-finance linkages. Indeed, a variety of new questions and issues have taken on a new urgency in the aftermath of the recent crisis.

5.3.1   Unspanned Macroeconomic Risks

Classic early work such as Ang and Piazzesi (2003) maintained the assumption that bond yields span macroeconomic risks. But just as bond yields may not span stochastic volatility, so too they may not span the full set of macroeconomic risks that determine term premia. The practical implication for DNS-style yield curve modeling is that macroeconomic variables may not impact yields simply as determinants of the three yield factors; rather, there may be additional direct effects. Hence, building on important work by Ludvigson and Ng (2009), attention is beginning to turn to unspanned macroeconomic risks. Joslin et al. (2010), for example, explore bond market risk premia using a no-arbitrage version of Diebold et al. (2006b) that allows for two-way causality between yield factors and macroeconomic variables. See also Cieslak and Pavola (2011).

5.3.2 The Zero Lower Bound

In the aftermath of the global financial crisis, short-term government bond yields in several countries fell essentially to their zero lower bound. Furthermore, moving forward with inflation fairly well contained at low levels in many countries, the zero lower bound on nominal yields may bind more often than in the past.

Interestingly, a very different force, the aging global population, may also work to keep global real yields near the zero lower bound for the foreseeable future. Indeed two demographic channels push in that direction. First, as regards real yields, as an emerging bulge of 40- and 50-year-olds saves aggressively for retirement, real yields will be depressed. Second, as regards inflation, older populations have relatively greater distaste for inflation, as they are creditors rather than debtors, providing strong political pressure for low inflation. Both the real-yield effect and the inflation effect promote lower nominal yields.

Because of the new relevance of the zero lower bound, some recent research has begun to explore the effectiveness of various available monetary policy tools in that environment, as in Hamilton and Wu (2010a). Unfortunately, however, the zero lower bound has received little attention in the yield curve literature. In the future it will be important to have arbitrage-free models that ensure nonnegative nominal yields. One route forward involves nonaffine models, as with the quadratic-Gaussian and quadratic-Wishart term-structure models of Ahn et al. (2002) and Gourieroux and Sufana (2003). Kim and Singleton (2012) take the nonaffine route, arguing that affine and nonnegative affine models don't fit well near the zero bound and prefer instead nonaffine models such as quadratic-Gaussian. Interestingly, they find that "Key for achieving [good fit] are that the state variables are correlated (non-diagonal feedback matrix) and that there is a state variable with zero loading in the short rate equation." The correlated-factor AFNS model has precisely that structure, although its affine nature evidently renders it too restrictive near the zero bound.

Another route forward involves more sophisticated affine models. One possibility is affine but non-Gaussian models, driven, for example, by nonnegative square-root processes as in Cox et al. (1985).[8] Another possibility, and a very appealing one, involves otherwise-traditional affine Gaussian models that nevertheless impose the zero lower bound. For example, Krippner (2011a) imposes the zero bound explicitly in those models by representing physical currency as call options on bonds. This approach generalizes AFNS, thereby facilitating imposition of the lower bound while maintaining the familiarity and tractability of AFNS.

5.3.3   Bond Supply and the Risk Premium

A second macro-finance issue highlighted in the financial crisis is the link between bond supply and the risk premium. In a standard asset pricing model, changes in the supply of long-term bonds do not affect bond prices. In particular, in a pricing model without heterogeneity or frictions, bond premia are determined by the risk characteristics of bonds and the risk aversion of investors, both of which are unaffected by bond supply. Put differently, changes in bond supply do not change aggregate risk in standard general equilibrium models. Instead they simply reassign it, resulting in a "Modigliani-Miller theorem for public finance," as emphasized in Wallace (1981) and Eggertsson and Woodford (2003) among many others.

---

[8] See also Collin-Dufresne et al. (2008) and Gabaix (2007).

Apparently contrasting with the theoretical benchmark of "no supply effects" is the empirical reality of the recent financial crisis. As short-term policy rates reached their effective lower bound, various central banks tried to lower longer-term yields by taking various unconventional balance sheet actions. Notably, the Bank of England and the Federal Reserve purchased significant amounts of longer-term debt securities in order to put downward pressure on longer-term yields in order to support economic growth. Using a variety of approaches, several studies have concluded that the Fed's purchases were effective in lowering yields below levels that otherwise would have prevailed.[9]

However, the underlying mechanism for the declines in long-term yields remains an open question. Based on the usual decomposition of long yields, central bank bond purchases could affect two elements: the term premium and average expected future short-term yields.

Consider first the term premium. It could have fallen because the central bank securities purchases reduced the aggregate amount of longer-term bonds and duration risk in private-sector portfolios—which is commonly referred to as the *portfolio balance channel*. Intuitively, in this channel, by reducing the supply of long-term bonds, the central bank shortens the average maturity of outstanding securities, and thus reduces aggregate duration risk. One might then expect that the risk or term premium associated with this duration risk would also decrease.

The theoretical underpinnings of the portfolio balance channel have been described by Vayanos and Vila (2009) and Hamilton and Wu (2010a). The crucial departure

---

[9] See D'Amico and King (2010), Gagnon et al. (2011), and Hamilton and Wu (2010a).

from a frictionless general equilibrium model is that bonds of different maturities are not perfect substitutes, that is, because some preferred-habitat investors have maturity-specific demand for bonds. In such a model with market segmentation, the maturity structure of outstanding debt affects the price of duration risk and thus risk premia.

Alternatively, now consider average expected future short-term yields. Purchases could have led market participants to revise down their expectations for future short-term interest rates, lengthening, for example, the expected period of a near-zero federal funds rate target. Such a *signaling channel* would reduce yields by lowering the risk-neutral component of long-term rates.

The relative importance of declines in the expectations and term premium components in accounting for declines in bond yields following central bank purchases remains unclear. Gagnon et al. (2011) examine this issue and conclude that the "reductions in interest rates primarily reflect lower risk premiums . . . rather than lower expectations of future short-term interest rates." They employ a conventional empirical dynamic term structure model to decompose long rates into risk-neutral rates and a term premium and then, in an event study, consider cumulative changes in interest rates and the term premium around important announcement dates related to asset purchase announcements. As a robustness exercise, Bauer and Rudebusch (2011) and Christensen and Rudebusch (2012) re-examine this issue, and they find that, in contrast, the signaling channel was also an important avenue of influence. Hence further research on understanding potential supply effects on bond yields from a macro-finance perspective remains an important research topic.

6

Epilogue

We begin with a bit of history, as what we have done in this book blends the old and the new. In particular, we sketch and contrast what we will call the "traditional" and "modern" approaches to yield curve modeling, to heighten our understanding of where and how DNS/AFNS fits.

Early on, bond markets were few and far between, so the term structure of bond yields remained a dormant issue. But as financial markets developed, and as economic theory and measurement advanced, issues related to the yield curve emerged as central in asset allocation, asset pricing, and risk management.

The earliest work effectively assumes perfect foresight, as in Bohm-Bawerk (1889). Building on that work, early interwar term-structure modeling typically allows for risk but assumes risk neutrality, as in Fisher (1930) and Keynes (1936), culminating in the classic expectations theory of Hicks (1946). Hicks's most basic theory, sometimes called the "traditional expectations theory," asserts that current forward rates equal expected future spot rates, in which case current long rates are simple averages of expected future spot rates.

An immediate implication of the traditional expectations theory is that the yield curve will be flat if spot rates are expected to remain unchanged.[1] This conflicts with the observed upward-sloping average yield curve and directs attention to the possibility of "term premia" that may separate forward rates from expected future spot rates. The first resulting variant of the traditional expectations theory is the "liquidity preference theory" of Hicks (1946). Hicks posited that lenders prefer short maturities, to avoid the risk associated with holding long-duration bonds, and that borrowers prefer long maturities, to lock in the cost of finance. Lenders then require and receive long-maturity premia from borrowers, producing an upward-sloping average yield curve.

Richer approximations to average yield curves, and time-varying conditional yield curves, soon followed.[2] In the "preferred habitat" or "market segmentation" theory of Modigliani and Sutch (1967), different agents prefer to borrow or lend in different regions of the curve. Depending on the distribution of agents among various preferred habitats, the curve can take many shapes, not just upward sloping. Moreover, the "slope factor" generated by preferred habitats can vary over time, as the distribution of agents among various preferred habitats can vary over time, for example, with the level of yields and/or with expected business conditions, as in Meiselman (1962), Kessel (1965), Van Horne (1965), and Nelson (1972).[3] Perhaps most notably in that tradition,

---

[1] This would occur, for example, if the spot rate is a martingale and expectations are formed rationally, in which case the optimal spot rate forecast at all horizons is "no change."

[2] In addition to theory, measurement also advanced rapidly during this time. High-quality yield curve data, for example, were constructed by Durand (1958) and Malkiel (1966), among others.

[3] The early literature's emphasis on linking term premia to yield levels evidently traces to Keynes (1936), pp. 201–202. Yield levels, however, are of course just one aspect of business conditions, and the key issue is relating term premia to broad business conditions.

Nelson (1972) identified expected spot rates using time-series models, subtracted them from current forward rates to get term premia, and then projected the term premia on business conditions indicators.

The "traditional" literature's concern with dynamic yield curve evolution is very much maintained in the "modern" literature, which in many respects began with Vasicek (1977), and which was significantly extended in classic subsequent contributions by Duffie and Kan (1996), Dai and Singleton (2000), Ang and Piazzesi (2003), among others. The modern literature, however, introduces a key distinguishing characteristic: explicit enforcement of absence of arbitrage.

Interestingly, DNS and AFNS in many respects bridge the traditional and modern literatures. DNS is the penultimate traditional model: explicitly stochastic, dynamic, parsimonious yet flexible, three-factor state-space structure, and so on. AFNS is a "modernized" DNS, explicitly imposing no-arbitrage while maintaining its other appealing features and empirical tractability.

Against this background, several questions emerge, all of which are presently incompletely resolved but very much evident in the evolving literature, related to the role of no-arbitrage constraints, empirical tractability of various approaches to arbitrage-free modeling, and whether and why the DNS/AFNS model is "special." So, in parallel to Chapter 1, in which we began this book with several questions, we now end with three.

6.1 Is Imposition of No-Arbitrage Helpful?

DNS fits well, so if market yields are arbitrage-free, then DNS should also be arbitrage-free, at least up to an accurate approximation. Hence it would appear intuitively that no-arbitrage restrictions, if imposed on DNS, would likely be largely nonbinding. Hence the implicit feeling in Diebold and Li (2006) and subsequent DNS work is that DNS's lack of imposition of no-arbitrage is not very important, and that attention is better focused on other matters, primarily how to extend DNS in creative ways.

The AFNS theory shows that not only intuition but also rigorous theory suggests that imposition of no-arbitrage restrictions is unlikely to improve DNS forecasts. In particular, as shown in the key Proposition AFNS of Chapter 3, although no-arbitrage strongly restricts risk-neutral dynamics, it puts *no* restrictions on physical dynamics. Instead, imposition of no-arbitrage delivers only yield-adjustment terms that vary with maturity but are constant over time.

Important subsequent work effectively extends the "predictive irrelevance" flavor of Proposition AFNS to the general context of maximally flexible canonical models. In particular, Duffee (2011a) and Joslin et al. (2011b) advance arguments for predictive irrelevance in general yields-only environments. Joslin et al. (2011a), moreover, extend those arguments to environments that include macroeconomic fundamentals.

Hence, and perhaps ironically, several literatures have in a sense come full circle. From a financial economic perspective, one might feel uncomfortable about arbitrage possibilities in various "traditional" models, so Vasicek (1977), Duffie and Kan (1996), and Dai and Singleton (2000) made them arbitrage-free. Similarly, one might feel uncomfortable simply fitting unrestricted vector autoregressions, so Ang and Piazzesi (2003) made them arbitrage-free. Finally, one might feel uncomfortable fitting unrestricted DNS, so Christensen et al. (2011a) made it arbitrage-free. Presumably for certain central tasks (e.g., pricing) one *should* feel uncomfortable with models that don't impose no-arbitrage, but the emerging theoretical recognition is that, for at least one central task (forecasting), imposition of no-arbitrage appears theoretically unlikely to help.[4]

We hasten to add, however, that as discussed in section 3.7, empirical work *has* sometimes found predictive gains from imposing no-arbitrage in DNS environments. Whether such gains are largely real (e.g., coming from the AFNS yield-adjustment term) or largely just good luck (e.g., sample selection across various yields at various times in various countries) remains to be seen, and we look forward to additional research. Perhaps the current best-practice recommendation should be always to work with AFNS, as it is almost as simple as DNS to estimate, and imposition of no-arbitrage is clearly important for many, if not all, tasks.

6.2 Is AFNS the Only Tractable $A_0(3)$ Model?

The short answer is "until recently, but interestingly, not anymore." In our view, the claim that, until very recently, AFNS was the *only* empirically tractable modern model is not exaggeration. In particular, the maximally flexible canonical $A_0(N)$ models have notoriously recalcitrant likelihood surfaces, notwithstanding the rarely published acknowledgments of such. In recent insightful work, Hamilton and Wu (2010b) summarize the situation well:

---

[4] We say "appears theoretically unlikely to help" as opposed to "cannot help" because the AFNS yield-adjustment term, despite its time constancy, *could* help forecasts. It might, for example, serve to provide a bias correction.

Buried in the footnotes of this literature and in the
practical experience of those who have used these
models are tremendous numerical challenges in estimating the necessary parameters from the data due
to highly non-linear and badly-behaved likelihood
surfaces.

They proceed to clarify the precise reason for the empirical nightmares associated with the canonical models,
showing in particular that three leading canonical models
are *unidentified*.[5]

In addition to $A_0(N)$ identification problems, there
appear to be $A_0(N)$ data-mining problems. In particular,
Duffee (2010) shows that most standard affine arbitrage-
free models with profligate parameterization (i.e., maximally flexible models) imply Sharpe ratios absurdly
higher than can actually be obtained in practice. It would
appear, then, that for several reasons the maximally flexible $A_0(N)$ models are ill-suited for empirical work, at
least as traditionally empirically implemented.

Fortunately, however, the recent work of Joslin et al.
(2011b) remedies the situation and opens important new
doors. They develop a well-behaved (among other things,
identified) family of Gaussian term structure models,
for which trustworthy estimation is very simple, just
as with AFNS. Moreover, it turns out that AFNS is a
nested special case of their canonical form, corresponding to three extra constraints relative to the maximally
flexible model, including a repeated eigenvalue in the
risk-neutral dynamic matrix K^Q.[6]

---

[5] See also Hamilton and Wu (2011).

[6] In related work, Siegel (2009) considers arbitrage-free models
for bond *prices* rather than yields. Several benefits accrue relative
to Duffie-Kan. The model admits a general closed-form solution,
and the drift is not affected by the diffusion, which simplifies the
incorporation of stochastic volatility. Roughly, then, it seems that

6.3 Is AFNS Special?

The obvious question, then, is whether AFNS, although clearly an important member and early discovery in what was later expanded to the Joslin et al. (2011b) class, continues to merit elevated status; that is, whether it is special in some way. There are many issues and nuances, and it is too soon to offer a definitive answer. Indeed there may never *be* a definitive answer, but in what follows we offer several insights that bear on the question. All told, we believe that AFNS *is* special, based on at least three classes of considerations.

6.3.1 AFNS's Simple Structure Facilitates Specializations, Extensions, and Varied Uses

AFNS's structure conveys several important and useful characteristics, which are presently difficult or impossible to achieve in competing frameworks. First, as regards specializations, its parametric simplicity makes it easy to impose restrictions. Second, as regards extensions, it is similarly easy to increase the number of AFNS latent factors, for example, with the five-factor AFGNS model of section 4.2.2.[7] Third, as regards varied uses, its flexible continuous basis functions facilitate relative pricing, curve interpolation between observed yields, and risk measurement for arbitrary bond portfolios.

Siegel's family is to discount curves what the Joslin et al. (2011b) family is to yield curves. Moreover, a specific member of Siegel's family parallels closely the AFNS yield model in structure, fit, and tractability.

[7]Krippner (2011b) tabulates and discusses a range of existing and potential extensions to the AFNS model, and he characterizes the relationship between each extension and the generic Gaussian affine arbitrage-free model, $A_0(N)$.

6.3.2 AFNS Has Strong Approximation-Theoretic Motivation

Nelson and Siegel (1987) originally motivated their functional form via solutions to second-order differential equations:

> A class of functions that readily generates the typical yield curve shapes is that associated with solutions to differential . . . equations . . . if the instantaneous forward rate . . . is given by the solution to a second-order differential equation with real and unequal roots, we would have . . . a family of forward rate curves that take on monotonic, humped, or S shapes . . . , and the implied yield curve displays the same range of shapes. (pp. 474–475)

Interestingly, moreover, Nelson and Siegel introduce a restriction that leads them to an explicit justification in terms of function approximation:

> A more parsimonious model that can generate the same range of shapes is given by the solution equation for the case of equal roots. . . . This model may also be derived as an approximation to the solution in the unequal roots case by expanding in a power series in the difference between the roots. . . . [It] may also be viewed as a constant plus a Laguerre function . . . [which is a] polynomial times an exponential decay term and is a mathematical class of approximating functions. (p. 475)

We note that the equal-root assumption is not unrelated to the repeated eigenvalue in the AFNS risk-neutral dynamic matrix K^Q.

Recent important work takes the function-approximation justification significantly further. In particular, Krippner (2011b) shows that the Nelson-Siegel form provides a Taylor-series approximation to arbitrary $A_0(N)$

term-structure dynamics. To be more precise, Krippner shows that the level, slope, and curvature components common to all Nelson-Siegel models arise explicitly from low-ordered Taylor-series expansions around central measures of the eigenvalues for the generic Gaussian affine term-structure model. Hence any yield curve from the $A_0(N)$ class can be approximated parsimoniously by an AFNS model.

6.3.3 AFNS Restrictions Are Not Rejected

As mentioned earlier, AFNS is a nested special case of the Joslin et al. (2011b) canonical form, corresponding to three restrictions. Hence likelihood-ratio and related tests of the AFNS null hypothesis are immediately applicable, and Joslin et al. (2011b) perform them. Interestingly, when they normalize their model such that their yield factors are the first three principal components—a natural and obvious benchmark in their view and ours—they find no evidence against AFNS.[8] We are not surprised by the nonrejection. Indeed, for the many reasons that we have emphasized throughout this book, we expect AFNS to fit well. Moreover, even if somehow rejected, we find it unlikely that AFNS would be far in any meaningful economic sense from an as-yet-unknown "preferred" three-factor model.

---

[8] Indeed the p-value of their likelihood-ratio test statistic is greater than 0.5.

Appendixes

Appendix A
Two-Factor AFNS Calculations

Here we provide details of two-factor AFNS calculations under risk aversion. Results under risk neutrality are of course included as a special case.

To derive the affine bond pricing formulas and yield curve equations, consider the case with prices of risk $\lambda_t = \left(\lambda_t^1 \ \ \lambda_t^2\right)'$. (Note that equation (3.9) can be obtained from (3.10) by setting the prices of risk to zero.) There are two ways to derive these formulas. First, we can construct a risk-neutral probability measure under which the risk-neutral pricing formula (3.7) holds. Second, we can start from the Euler equation $E\left[d(m_t F_t)\right] = 0$. We consider each in turn.

A.1   Risk-Neutral Probability

Under the risk-neutral probability measure, the process B^* that solves $dB_t^* = dB_t + \lambda_t dt$ is a Brownian motion. By solving for dB_t and inserting this expression into the AR(1) dynamics of the factors (3.6), we get

$$
\begin{aligned}
dx_t^i &= \kappa_i(\theta_i - x_t^i)dt + \sigma_i(dB_t^{*i} - \lambda_t^i dt) \\
&= \left(\kappa_i\theta_i - \kappa_i x_t^i - \sigma_i\lambda_0^i - \sigma_i\lambda_1^i x_t^i\right) dt + \sigma_i dB_t^{*i} \\
&= \left(\kappa_i\theta_i - \sigma_i\lambda_0^i - (\kappa_i + \sigma_i\lambda_1^i)x_t^i\right) dt + \sigma_i dB_t^{*i}
\end{aligned}
$$

$$= (\kappa_i + \sigma_i \lambda_1^i) \left(\frac{\kappa_i \theta_i - \sigma_i \lambda_0^i}{(\kappa_i + \sigma_i \lambda_1^i)} - x_t^i \right) dt + \sigma_i dB_t^{*i}$$

$$= \kappa_i^* \left(\theta_i^* - x_t^i \right) dt + \sigma_i dB_t^{*i},$$

where

$$\kappa_i^* = \kappa_i + \sigma_i \lambda_1^i,$$

$$\theta_i^* = \frac{\kappa_i \theta_i - \sigma_i \lambda_0^i}{\kappa_i + \sigma_i \lambda_1^i}.$$

The price of the τ-period bond is

$$P_t^{(\tau)} = E_t^* \left(\exp \left(- \int_t^{t+\tau} r_s ds \right) \right),$$

where the expectations operator E^* uses the risk-neutral probability measure. Since the vector $x = (x_1, x_2)'$ is Markov, this expectation is a function of the state today x_t. Hence the bond price is a function $P_t^{(\tau)} = F(x_t, \tau)$ of the state vector x_t and time-to-maturity τ. By the Feynman-Kac formula, F solves the partial differential equation

$$F_t r_t = - \frac{\partial F}{\partial \tau} + \sum_{i=1}^2 \left[\frac{\partial F}{\partial x^i} \kappa_i^* \left(\theta_i^* - x_t^i \right) + \frac{1}{2} \frac{\partial^2 F}{\partial x^{i2}} \sigma_i^2 \right],$$

with terminal condition $F(x, 0) = 1$.

We guess the solution

$$F(x_t, \tau) = \exp \left(A(\tau) + B(\tau) x_t \right), \qquad \text{(A.1)}$$

which means that

$$\frac{\partial F}{\partial x^i} = B_i(\tau) F,$$

$$\frac{\partial^2 F}{\partial x^{i2}} = B_i(\tau)^2 F,$$

$$\frac{\partial F}{\partial \tau} = \left(A'(\tau) + B'(\tau) x_t \right) F.$$

Inserting these expressions into the partial differential equation, we obtain

$$x_t^1 + x_t^2 = -A'(\tau) - B_1'(\tau)x_t^1 - B_2'(\tau)x_t^2$$
$$+ \sum_{i=1}^{2}[B_i(\tau)\kappa_i^*(\theta_i^* - x_t^i) + \tfrac{1}{2}B_i(\tau)^2\sigma_i^2].$$

Matching coefficients produces

$$A'(\tau) = \sum_{i=1}^{2} B_i(\tau)\kappa_i^*\theta_i^* + \tfrac{1}{2}B_i(\tau)^2\sigma_i^2,$$
$$1 = -B_1'(\tau) - B_1(\tau)\kappa_1^*,$$
$$1 = -B_2'(\tau) - B_2(\tau)\kappa_2^*.$$

The boundary conditions are

$$A(0) = 0 \quad \text{and} \quad B(0) = 0_{2\times 1}.$$

These ODEs have solutions

$$B_1(\tau) = \frac{(\exp(-\kappa_1^*\tau) - 1)}{\kappa_1^*}, \tag{A.2}$$
$$B_2(\tau) = \frac{(\exp(-\kappa_2^*\tau) - 1)}{\kappa_2^*},$$

and inserting them into the yield equation produces

$$y_t^{(\tau)} = -\frac{A(\tau)}{\tau} - \frac{B_1(\tau)}{\tau}x_t^1 - \frac{B_2(\tau)}{\tau}x_t^2$$
$$= a^{NA}(\tau) + b_1^{NA}(\tau)x_t^1 + b_2^{NA}(\tau)x_t^2,$$

which is equation (3.9).

A.2   Euler Equation

The Euler equation is

$$P_t^{(\tau)} = E_t\left[\frac{m_{t+\tau}}{m_t}\right],$$

and the instantaneous equation is

$$E\left[d(m_t F_t)\right] = 0. \tag{A.3}$$

The bond price is a function $F(x, \tau)$. Application of Ito's lemma produces

$$dF = \mu_F dt + \sigma_F dB_t,$$

where the drift and volatility are

$$\mu_F = -\frac{\partial F}{\partial \tau} + \sum_{i=1}^{2} \left[\frac{\partial F}{\partial x_i} \kappa_i \left(\theta_i - x^i\right) + \frac{1}{2} \frac{\partial^2 F}{\partial x^{i2}} \sigma_i^2 \right],$$

$$\sigma_F = \sum_{i=1}^{2} \frac{\partial F}{\partial x^i} \sigma_i.$$

Both m_t and F_t are Ito processes, so their product solves

$$d(m_t F_t) = -r_t m_t F_t dt + m_t \mu_t^F dt - m_t \lambda_t \sigma_t^F dt$$
$$- F_t m_t \lambda_t dB_t + m_t \sigma_t^F dB_t.$$

Using the Euler equation (A.3), we obtain

$$0 = -r_t m_t F_t + m_t \mu_t^F - m_t \lambda_t \sigma_t^F, \tag{A.4}$$

$$F_t r_t = \left(-\frac{\partial F}{\partial \tau} + \sum_{i=1}^{2} \left[\frac{\partial F}{\partial x^i} \kappa_i (\theta_i - x_t^i) + \frac{1}{2} \frac{\partial^2 F}{\partial x^{i2}} \sigma_i^2 \right] \right)$$
$$- \sum_{i=1}^{2} \frac{\partial F}{\partial x^i} \sigma_i \lambda_t^i.$$

Again we guess the exponential-affine solution (A.1) and insert the expressions into (A.4) to obtain

$$x_t^1 + x_t^2 = -A'(\tau) - B_1'(\tau)x_t^1 - B_2'(\tau)x_t^2$$
$$+ \sum_{i=1}^{2}[B_i(\tau)\kappa_i(\theta_i - x_t^i) + \tfrac{1}{2}B_i(\tau)^2\sigma_i^2]$$
$$- \sum_{i=1}^{2} B_i(\tau)\sigma_i(\lambda_0^i + \lambda_1^i x_t^i).$$

Matching coefficients produces the ordinary differential equations:

$$A'(\tau) = \sum_{i=1}^{2} B_i(\tau)(\kappa_i\theta_i - \sigma_i\lambda_0^i) + \tfrac{1}{2}B_i(\tau)^2\sigma_i^2,$$
$$1 = -B_1'(\tau) - B_1(\tau)(\kappa_1 + \sigma_1\lambda_1^1),$$
$$1 = -B_2'(\tau) - B_2(\tau)(\kappa_2 + \sigma_2\lambda_1^2).$$

Hence we obtain the coefficients (A.2) with risk-neutral parameters. That is,

$$\kappa_i^* = \kappa_i + \sigma_i\lambda_1^i,$$
$$\kappa_i^*\theta_i^* = \kappa_i\theta_i - \sigma_i\lambda_0^i,$$

so that

$$\theta_i^* = \frac{\kappa_i\theta_i - \sigma_i\lambda_0^i}{\kappa_i + \sigma_i\lambda_1^i}.$$

Appendix B

Details of AFNS Restrictions

Here we provide details of the AFNS restrictions on $A_0(3)$, as calculated using the theory of affine-invariant transformations.

Derivation of the AFNS restrictions imposed on the canonical representation of the $A_0(3)$ class starts with an arbitrary affine diffusion process represented by

$$dY_t = K_Y^Q[\theta_Y^Q - Y_t]dt + \Sigma_Y dW_t^Q.$$

Now consider the affine transformation $\mathcal{T}_Y : AY_t + \eta$, where A is a nonsingular square matrix of the same dimension as Y_t and η is a vector of constants of the same dimension as Y_t. Denote the transformed process by $X_t = AY_t + \eta$. By Ito's lemma it follows that

$$
\begin{aligned}
dX_t &= AdY_t \\
&= [AK_Y^Q\theta_Y^Q - AK_Y^QY_t]dt + A\Sigma_Y dW_t^Q \\
&= AK_Y^QA^{-1}[A\theta_Y^Q - AY_t - \eta + \eta]dt + A\Sigma_Y dW_t^Q \\
&= AK_Y^QA^{-1}[A\theta_Y^Q + \eta - X_t]dt + A\Sigma_Y dW_t^Q \\
&= K_X^Q[\theta_X^Q - X_t]dt + \Sigma_X dW_t^Q.
\end{aligned}
$$

Thus X_t is itself an affine diffusion process with parameters $K_X^Q = AK_Y^QA^{-1}$, $\theta_X^Q = A\theta_Y^Q + \eta$, and $\Sigma_X = A\Sigma_Y$. A similar result holds for the dynamics under the P-measure.

For the short-rate process we have

$$
\begin{aligned}
r_t &= \delta_0^Y + (\delta_1^Y)' Y_t \\
&= \delta_0^Y + (\delta_1^Y)'^{-1} A Y_t \\
&= \delta_0^Y + (\delta_1^Y)'^{-1} [A Y_t + \eta - \eta] \\
&= \delta_0^Y - (\delta_1^Y)'^{-1} \eta + (\delta_1^Y)'^{-1} X_t.
\end{aligned}
$$

Thus, defining

$$
\delta_0^X = \delta_0^Y - (\delta_1^Y)'^{-1} \eta
$$

and

$$
\delta_1^X = (\delta_1^Y)'^{-1},
$$

the short-rate process is unchanged and may be represented either as

$$
r_t = \delta_0^Y + (\delta_1^Y)' Y_t
$$

or as

$$
r_t = \delta_0^X + (\delta_1^X)' X_t.
$$

Because both Y_t and X_t are affine latent factor processes that deliver the same distribution for the short-rate process r_t, they are equivalent representations of the same fundamental model; hence $\mathcal{T}_X$ is called an affine invariant transformation.

In the canonical representation of the subset of $A_0(3)$ affine term structure models considered here, the Q-dynamics are

$$
\begin{pmatrix} dY_t^1 \\ dY_t^2 \\ dY_t^3 \end{pmatrix} = - \begin{pmatrix} \kappa_{11}^{Y,Q} & \kappa_{12}^{Y,Q} & \kappa_{13}^{Y,Q} \\ 0 & \kappa_{22}^{Y,Q} & \kappa_{23}^{Y,Q} \\ 0 & 0 & \kappa_{33}^{Y,Q} \end{pmatrix} \begin{pmatrix} Y_t^1 \\ Y_t^2 \\ Y_t^3 \end{pmatrix} dt
$$

$$
+ \begin{pmatrix} 1 & 0 & 0 \\ 0 & 1 & 0 \\ 0 & 0 & 1 \end{pmatrix} \begin{pmatrix} dW_t^{1,Q} \\ dW_t^{2,Q} \\ dW_t^{3,Q} \end{pmatrix},
$$

the P-dynamics are

$$\begin{pmatrix} dY_t^1 \\ dY_t^2 \\ dY_t^3 \end{pmatrix} = \begin{pmatrix} \kappa_{11}^{Y,P} & \kappa_{12}^{Y,P} & \kappa_{13}^{Y,P} \\ \kappa_{21}^{Y,P} & \kappa_{22}^{Y,P} & \kappa_{23}^{Y,P} \\ \kappa_{31}^{Y,P} & \kappa_{32}^{Y,P} & \kappa_{33}^{Y,P} \end{pmatrix} \left[\begin{pmatrix} \theta_1^{Y,P} \\ \theta_2^{Y,P} \\ \theta_3^{Y,P} \end{pmatrix} - \begin{pmatrix} Y_t^1 \\ Y_t^2 \\ Y_t^3 \end{pmatrix} \right] dt$$
$$+ \begin{pmatrix} 1 & 0 & 0 \\ 0 & 1 & 0 \\ 0 & 0 & 1 \end{pmatrix} \begin{pmatrix} dW_t^{1,P} \\ dW_t^{2,P} \\ dW_t^{3,P} \end{pmatrix},$$

and the instantaneous risk-free rate is

$$r_t = \delta_0^Y + \delta_{1,1}^Y Y_t^1 + \delta_{1,2}^Y Y_t^2 + \delta_{1,3}^Y Y_t^3.$$

There are 22 parameters in this maximally flexible canonical representation of the $A_0(3)$ class of models, and here we present the parameter restrictions needed to arrive at the affine AFNS models.

B.1   Independent-Factor AFNS

The independent-factor AFNS model has P-dynamics

$$\begin{pmatrix} dX_t^1 \\ dX_t^2 \\ dX_t^3 \end{pmatrix} = \begin{pmatrix} \kappa_{11}^{X,P} & 0 & 0 \\ 0 & \kappa_{22}^{X,P} & 0 \\ 0 & 0 & \kappa_{33}^{X,P} \end{pmatrix} \left[\begin{pmatrix} \theta_1^{X,P} \\ \theta_2^{X,P} \\ \theta_3^{X,P} \end{pmatrix} - \begin{pmatrix} X_t^1 \\ X_t^2 \\ X_t^3 \end{pmatrix} \right] dt$$
$$+ \begin{pmatrix} \sigma_{11}^X & 0 & 0 \\ 0 & \sigma_{22}^X & 0 \\ 0 & 0 & \sigma_{33}^X \end{pmatrix} \begin{pmatrix} dW_t^{1,P} \\ dW_t^{2,P} \\ dW_t^{3,P} \end{pmatrix},$$

and the Q-dynamics are given by Proposition AFNS as

$$
\begin{pmatrix} dX_t^1 \\ dX_t^2 \\ dX_t^3 \end{pmatrix} = - \begin{pmatrix} 0 & 0 & 0 \\ 0 & \lambda & -\lambda \\ 0 & 0 & \lambda \end{pmatrix} \begin{pmatrix} X_t^1 \\ X_t^2 \\ X_t^3 \end{pmatrix} dt
$$
$$
+ \begin{pmatrix} \sigma_{11}^X & 0 & 0 \\ 0 & \sigma_{22}^X & 0 \\ 0 & 0 & \sigma_{33}^X \end{pmatrix} \begin{pmatrix} dW_t^{1,Q} \\ dW_t^{2,Q} \\ dW_t^{3,Q} \end{pmatrix}.
$$

Finally, the short-rate process is $r_t = X_t^1 + X_t^2$. This model has a total of 10 parameters; thus 12 parameter restrictions need to be imposed on the canonical $A_0(3)$ model.

It is easy to verify that the affine invariant transformation

$$
\mathcal{T}_A(Y_t) = AY_t + \eta
$$

will convert the canonical representation into the independent-factor AFNS model, where

$$
A = \begin{pmatrix} \sigma_{11}^X & 0 & 0 \\ 0 & \sigma_{22}^X & 0 \\ 0 & 0 & \sigma_{33}^X \end{pmatrix}
$$

and $\eta = (0 \ 0 \ 0)'$. For the mean-reversion matrices, we have $K_X^P = AK_Y^P A^{-1}$, which is equivalent to $K_Y^P = A^{-1}K_X^P A$, and $K_X^Q = AK_Y^Q A^{-1}$, which is equivalent to $K_Y^Q = A^{-1}K_X^Q A$. The equivalent mean-reversion matrix under the Q-measure is then

$$
K_Y^Q = \begin{pmatrix} \dfrac{1}{\sigma_{11}^X} & 0 & 0 \\ 0 & \dfrac{1}{\sigma_{22}^X} & 0 \\ 0 & 0 & \dfrac{1}{\sigma_{33}^X} \end{pmatrix} \begin{pmatrix} 0 & 0 & 0 \\ 0 & \lambda & -\lambda \\ 0 & 0 & \lambda \end{pmatrix} \begin{pmatrix} \sigma_{11}^X & 0 & 0 \\ 0 & \sigma_{22}^X & 0 \\ 0 & 0 & \sigma_{33}^X \end{pmatrix}
$$

$$= \begin{pmatrix} 0 & 0 & 0 \\ 0 & \lambda & -\lambda\dfrac{\sigma^X_{33}}{\sigma^X_{22}} \\ 0 & 0 & \lambda \end{pmatrix}.$$

Thus four restrictions need to be imposed on the upper triangular mean-reversion matrix K^Q_Y:

$$K^{Y,Q}_{11} = 0, \quad K^{Y,Q}_{12} = 0, \quad K^{Y,Q}_{13} = 0, \quad K^{Y,Q}_{33} = K^Y_{22}.$$

Furthermore, notice that the sign of $K^{Y,Q}_{23}$ will always be the opposite to that of both $K^{Y,Q}_{22}$ and $K^{Y,Q}_{33}$, but its absolute size can vary independently of these two parameters. Because K^P_X, A, and A^{-1} are all diagonal matrices, K^P_Y is a diagonal matrix, too. This gives another six restrictions.

Finally, we can study the factor loadings in the affine function for the short-rate process. In all AFNS models, $r_t = X^1_t + X^2_t$, which is equivalent to fixing $\delta^X_0 = 0$ and $\delta^X_1 = (1 \ 1 \ 0)'$. From the relation $(\delta^X_1)' = (\delta^Y_1)'^{-1}$ it follows that

$$\begin{aligned} (\delta^Y_1)' &= (\delta^X_1)'A \\ &= (1 \ 1 \ 0) \begin{pmatrix} \sigma^X_{11} & 0 & 0 \\ 0 & \sigma^X_{22} & 0 \\ 0 & 0 & \sigma^X_{33} \end{pmatrix} \\ &= (\sigma^X_{11} \ \sigma^X_{22} \ 0). \end{aligned}$$

For the constant term we have

$$\delta^X_0 = \delta^Y_0 - (\delta^Y_1)'^{-1}\eta,$$

which is equivalent to $\delta^Y_0 = \delta^X_0 = 0$. Thus we have obtained two additional parameter restrictions, $\delta^Y_0 = 0$ and $\delta^Y_{1,3} = 0$.

B.2   Correlated-Factor AFNS

In the correlated-factor AFNS model, the P-dynamics
are

$$
\begin{pmatrix} dX_t^1 \\ dX_t^2 \\ dX_t^3 \end{pmatrix} = \begin{pmatrix} \kappa_{11}^{X,P} & \kappa_{12}^{X,P} & \kappa_{13}^{X,P} \\ \kappa_{21}^{X,P} & \kappa_{22}^{X,P} & \kappa_{23}^{X,P} \\ \kappa_{31}^{X,P} & \kappa_{32}^{X,P} & \kappa_{33}^{X,P} \end{pmatrix} \left[\begin{pmatrix} \theta_1^{X,P} \\ \theta_2^{X,P} \\ \theta_3^{X,P} \end{pmatrix} - \begin{pmatrix} X_t^1 \\ X_t^2 \\ X_t^3 \end{pmatrix} \right] dt
$$

$$
+ \begin{pmatrix} \sigma_{11}^X & \sigma_{12}^X & \sigma_{13}^X \\ 0 & \sigma_{22}^X & \sigma_{23}^X \\ 0 & 0 & \sigma_{33}^X \end{pmatrix} \begin{pmatrix} dW_t^{1,P} \\ dW_t^{2,P} \\ dW_t^{3,P} \end{pmatrix},
$$

and the Q-dynamics are given by Proposition AFNS as

$$
\begin{pmatrix} dX_t^1 \\ dX_t^2 \\ dX_t^3 \end{pmatrix} = - \begin{pmatrix} 0 & 0 & 0 \\ 0 & \lambda & -\lambda \\ 0 & 0 & \lambda \end{pmatrix} \begin{pmatrix} X_t^1 \\ X_t^2 \\ X_t^3 \end{pmatrix} dt
$$

$$
+ \begin{pmatrix} \sigma_{11}^X & \sigma_{12}^X & \sigma_{13}^X \\ 0 & \sigma_{22}^X & \sigma_{23}^X \\ 0 & 0 & \sigma_{33}^X \end{pmatrix} \begin{pmatrix} dW_t^{1,Q} \\ dW_t^{2,Q} \\ dW_t^{3,Q} \end{pmatrix}.
$$

This model has a total of 19 parameters; thus three
parameter restrictions are needed.

It is easy to verify that the affine invariant transformation $\mathcal{T}_A(Y_t) = AY_t + \eta$ will convert the canonical
representation into the correlated-factor AFNS model
when

$$
A = \begin{pmatrix} \sigma_{11}^X & \sigma_{12}^X & \sigma_{13}^X \\ 0 & \sigma_{22}^X & \sigma_{23}^X \\ 0 & 0 & \sigma_{33}^X \end{pmatrix}
$$

and $\eta = (0\ 0\ 0)'$. For the mean-reversion matrices, we have $K_X^P = AK_Y^P A^{-1}$, which is equivalent to $K_Y^P = A^{-1}K_X^P A$, and $K_X^Q = AK_Y^Q A^{-1}$, which is equivalent to $K_Y^Q = A^{-1}K_X^Q A$. The equivalent mean-reversion matrix under the Q-measure is then

$$
K_Y^Q = \begin{pmatrix} \dfrac{1}{\sigma_{11}^X} & -\dfrac{\sigma_{12}^X}{\sigma_{11}^X\sigma_{22}^X} & -\left(\dfrac{\sigma_{13}^X}{\sigma_{11}^X\sigma_{33}^X} - \dfrac{\sigma_{12}^X\sigma_{23}^X}{\sigma_{11}^X\sigma_{22}^X\sigma_{33}^X}\right) \\[3ex] 0 & \dfrac{1}{\sigma_{22}^X} & -\dfrac{\sigma_{23}^X}{\sigma_{22}^X\sigma_{33}^X} \\[3ex] 0 & 0 & \dfrac{1}{\sigma_{33}^X} \end{pmatrix}
$$

$$
\times \begin{pmatrix} 0 & 0 & 0 \\ 0 & \lambda & -\lambda \\ 0 & 0 & \lambda \end{pmatrix} \begin{pmatrix} \sigma_{11}^X & \sigma_{12}^X & \sigma_{13}^X \\ 0 & \sigma_{22}^X & \sigma_{23}^X \\ 0 & 0 & \sigma_{33}^X \end{pmatrix}
$$

$$
= \begin{pmatrix} 0 & -\lambda\dfrac{\sigma_{12}^X}{\sigma_{11}^X} & \lambda\dfrac{\sigma_{12}^X\sigma_{33}^X - \sigma_{22}^X\sigma_{13}^X}{\sigma_{11}^X\sigma_{22}^X} \\[3ex] 0 & \lambda & -\lambda\dfrac{\sigma_{33}^X}{\sigma_{22}^X} \\[3ex] 0 & 0 & \lambda \end{pmatrix}.
$$

Thus two restrictions need to be imposed on the upper triangular mean-reversion matrix K_Y^Q: $K_{11}^{Y,Q} = 0$ and $K_{33}^{Y,Q} = K_{22}^{Y,Q}$. Furthermore, notice that $K_{23}^{Y,Q}$ will always have the opposite sign of $K_{22}^{Y,Q}$ and $K_{33}^{Y,Q}$, but its absolute size can vary independently of the two other parameters.

Next we study the factor loadings in the affine function for the short-rate process. In the AFNS models, $r_t = X_t^1 + X_t^2$, which is equivalent to fixing $\delta_0^X = 0$ and $\delta_1^X = (1\ 1\ 0)'$. From the relation $(\delta_1^X)' = (\delta_1^Y)'^{-1}$, it follows that

$$(\delta_1^Y)' = (\delta_1^X)'A$$

$$= \begin{pmatrix} 1 & 1 & 0 \end{pmatrix} \begin{pmatrix} \sigma_{11}^X & \sigma_{12}^X & \sigma_{13}^X \\ 0 & \sigma_{22}^X & \sigma_{23}^X \\ 0 & 0 & \sigma_{33}^X \end{pmatrix}$$

$$= \begin{pmatrix} \sigma_{11}^X & \sigma_{21}^X + \sigma_{22}^X & \sigma_{13}^X + \sigma_{23}^X \end{pmatrix}.$$

This shows that there are no restrictions on δ_1^Y. For the constant term, we have $\delta_0^X = \delta_0^Y - (\delta_1^Y)'^{-1}\eta$, which is equivalent to $\delta_0^Y = \delta_0^X = 0$. Thus we obtain one additional parameter restriction, $\delta_0^Y = 0$. Finally, for the mean-reversion matrix under the P-measure, we have $K_X^P = AK_Y^PA^{-1}$, which is equivalent to $K_Y^P = A^{-1}K_X^PA$. Because K_X^P is a free 3×3 matrix, K_Y^P is also a free 3×3 matrix. Thus no restrictions are imposed on the P-dynamics in the equivalent canonical representation of this model.

Appendix C
The AFGNS Yield-Adjustment Term

Given a general volatility matrix

$$\Sigma = \begin{pmatrix} \sigma_{11} & \sigma_{12} & \sigma_{13} & \sigma_{14} & \sigma_{15} \\ \sigma_{21} & \sigma_{22} & \sigma_{23} & \sigma_{24} & \sigma_{25} \\ \sigma_{31} & \sigma_{32} & \sigma_{33} & \sigma_{34} & \sigma_{35} \\ \sigma_{41} & \sigma_{42} & \sigma_{43} & \sigma_{44} & \sigma_{45} \\ \sigma_{51} & \sigma_{52} & \sigma_{53} & \sigma_{54} & \sigma_{55} \end{pmatrix},$$

the analytical AFGNS yield-adjustment term is

$$
\begin{aligned}
\frac{C(t,T)}{T-t} &= \frac{1}{2}\frac{1}{T-t}\int_t^T \sum_{j=1}^5 \left(\Sigma' B(s,T)B(s,T)'\Sigma\right)_{j,j} ds \\
&= \bar{A}\frac{(T-t)^2}{6} \\
&\quad + \bar{B}\left[\frac{1}{2\lambda_1^2} - \frac{1}{\lambda_1^3}\frac{1-e^{-\lambda_1(T-t)}}{T-t} + \frac{1}{4\lambda_1^3}\frac{1-e^{-2\lambda_1(T-t)}}{T-t}\right] \\
&\quad + \bar{C}\left[\frac{1}{2\lambda_2^2} - \frac{1}{\lambda_2^3}\frac{1-e^{-\lambda_2(T-t)}}{T-t} + \frac{1}{4\lambda_2^3}\frac{1-e^{-2\lambda_2(T-t)}}{T-t}\right]
\end{aligned}
$$

$$+ \bar{D}\left[\frac{1}{2\lambda_1^2} + \frac{1}{\lambda_1^2}e^{-\lambda_1(T-t)} - \frac{1}{4\lambda_1}(T-t)e^{-2\lambda_1(T-t)}\right.$$

$$- \frac{3}{4\lambda_1^2}e^{-2\lambda_1(T-t)} + \frac{5}{8\lambda_1^3}\frac{1 - e^{-2\lambda_1(T-t)}}{T-t}$$

$$\left. - \frac{2}{\lambda_1^3}\frac{1 - e^{-\lambda_1(T-t)}}{T-t}\right]$$

$$+ \bar{E}\left[\frac{1}{2\lambda_2^2} + \frac{1}{\lambda_2^2}e^{-\lambda_2(T-t)} - \frac{1}{4\lambda_2}(T-t)e^{-2\lambda_2(T-t)}\right.$$

$$- \frac{3}{4\lambda_2^2}e^{-2\lambda_2(T-t)} + \frac{5}{8\lambda_2^3}\frac{1 - e^{-2\lambda_2(T-t)}}{T-t}$$

$$\left. - \frac{2}{\lambda_2^3}\frac{1 - e^{-\lambda_2(T-t)}}{T-t}\right]$$

$$+ \bar{F}\left[\frac{1}{2\lambda_1}(T-t) + \frac{1}{\lambda_1^2}e^{-\lambda_1(T-t)} - \frac{1}{\lambda_1^3}\frac{1 - e^{-\lambda_1(T-t)}}{T-t}\right]$$

$$+ \bar{G}\left[\frac{1}{2\lambda_2}(T-t) + \frac{1}{\lambda_2^2}e^{-\lambda_2(T-t)} - \frac{1}{\lambda_2^3}\frac{1 - e^{-\lambda_2(T-t)}}{T-t}\right]$$

$$+ \bar{H}\left[\frac{3}{\lambda_1^2}e^{-\lambda_1(T-t)} + \frac{1}{2\lambda_1}(T-t)\right.$$

$$\left. + \frac{1}{\lambda_1}(T-t)e^{-\lambda_1(T-t)} - \frac{3}{\lambda_1^3}\frac{1 - e^{-\lambda_1(T-t)}}{T-t}\right]$$

$$+ \bar{I}\left[\frac{3}{\lambda_2^2}e^{-\lambda_2(T-t)} + \frac{1}{2\lambda_2}(T-t) + \frac{1}{\lambda_2}(T-t)e^{-\lambda_2(T-t)}\right.$$

$$\left. - \frac{3}{\lambda_2^3}\frac{1 - e^{-\lambda_2(T-t)}}{T-t}\right]$$

$$+ \bar{J}\left[\frac{1}{\lambda_1\lambda_2} - \frac{1}{\lambda_1^2\lambda_2}\frac{1 - e^{-\lambda_1(T-t)}}{T-t} - \frac{1}{\lambda_1\lambda_2^2}\frac{1 - e^{-\lambda_2(T-t)}}{T-t}\right.$$

$$\left. + \frac{1}{\lambda_1\lambda_2(\lambda_1 + \lambda_2)}\frac{1 - e^{-(\lambda_1+\lambda_2)(T-t)}}{T-t}\right]$$

$$+ \bar{K}\left[\frac{1}{\lambda_1^2} + \frac{1}{\lambda_1^2}e^{-\lambda_1(T-t)} - \frac{1}{2\lambda_1^2}e^{-2\lambda_1(T-t)}\right.$$

$$\left. - \frac{3}{\lambda_1^3}\frac{1-e^{-\lambda_1(T-t)}}{T-t} + \frac{3}{4\lambda_1^3}\frac{1-e^{-2\lambda_1(T-t)}}{T-t}\right]$$

$$+ \bar{L}\left[\frac{1}{\lambda_1\lambda_2} + \frac{1}{\lambda_1\lambda_2}e^{-\lambda_2(T-t)}\right.$$

$$- \frac{1}{\lambda_1(\lambda_1+\lambda_2)}e^{-(\lambda_1+\lambda_2)(T-t)}$$

$$- \frac{1}{\lambda_1^2\lambda_2}\frac{1-e^{-\lambda_1(T-t)}}{T-t} - \frac{2}{\lambda_1\lambda_2^2}\frac{1-e^{-\lambda_2(T-t)}}{T-t}$$

$$\left. + \frac{\lambda_1+2\lambda_2}{\lambda_1\lambda_2(\lambda_1+\lambda_2)^2}\left[1 - e^{-(\lambda_1+\lambda_2)(T-t)}\right]\right]$$

$$+ \bar{M}\left[\frac{1}{\lambda_1\lambda_2} + \frac{1}{\lambda_1\lambda_2}e^{-\lambda_1(T-t)}\right.$$

$$- \frac{1}{\lambda_2(\lambda_1+\lambda_2)}e^{-(\lambda_1+\lambda_2)(T-t)}$$

$$- \frac{1}{\lambda_1\lambda_2^2}\frac{1-e^{-\lambda_2(T-t)}}{T-t} - \frac{2}{\lambda_1^2\lambda_2}\frac{1-e^{-\lambda_1(T-t)}}{T-t}$$

$$\left. + \frac{\lambda_2+2\lambda_1}{\lambda_1\lambda_2(\lambda_1+\lambda_2)^2}\left[1 - e^{-(\lambda_1+\lambda_2)(T-t)}\right]\right]$$

$$+ \bar{N}\left[\frac{1}{\lambda_2^2} + \frac{1}{\lambda_2^2}e^{-\lambda_2(T-t)} - \frac{1}{2\lambda_2^2}e^{-2\lambda_2(T-t)}\right.$$

$$\left. - \frac{3}{\lambda_2^3}\frac{1-e^{-\lambda_2(T-t)}}{T-t} + \frac{3}{4\lambda_2^3}\frac{1-e^{-2\lambda_2(T-t)}}{T-t}\right]$$

$$+ \bar{O}\left[\frac{1}{\lambda_1\lambda_2} + \frac{1}{\lambda_1\lambda_2}e^{-\lambda_1(T-t)} + \frac{1}{\lambda_1\lambda_2}e^{-\lambda_2(T-t)}\right.$$

$$- \left(\frac{1}{\lambda_1} + \frac{1}{\lambda_2}\right)\frac{1}{\lambda_1+\lambda_2}e^{-(\lambda_1+\lambda_2)(T-t)}$$

$$- \frac{2}{(\lambda_1+\lambda_2)^2}e^{-(\lambda_1+\lambda_2)(T-t)}$$

$$- \frac{1}{\lambda_1 + \lambda_2}(T - t)e^{-(\lambda_1 + \lambda_2)(T-t)}$$

$$- \frac{2}{\lambda_1^2 \lambda_2}\frac{1 - e^{-\lambda_1(T-t)}}{T - t} - \frac{2}{\lambda_1 \lambda_2^2}\frac{1 - e^{-\lambda_2(T-t)}}{T - t}$$

$$+ \frac{2}{(\lambda_1 + \lambda_2)^3}\frac{1 - e^{-(\lambda_1 + \lambda_2)(T-t)}}{T - t}$$

$$+ \left(\frac{1}{\lambda_1} + \frac{1}{\lambda_2}\right)\frac{1}{(\lambda_1 + \lambda_2)^2}\frac{1 - e^{-(\lambda_1 + \lambda_2)(T-t)}}{T - t}$$

$$+ \frac{1}{\lambda_1 \lambda_2 (\lambda_1 + \lambda_2)}\frac{1 - e^{-(\lambda_1 + \lambda_2)(T-t)}}{T - t}\Bigg],$$

where

$$\bar{A} = \sigma_{11}^2 + \sigma_{12}^2 + \sigma_{13}^2 + \sigma_{14}^2 + \sigma_{15}^2,$$
$$\bar{B} = \sigma_{21}^2 + \sigma_{22}^2 + \sigma_{23}^2 + \sigma_{24}^2 + \sigma_{25}^2,$$
$$\bar{C} = \sigma_{31}^2 + \sigma_{32}^2 + \sigma_{33}^2 + \sigma_{34}^2 + \sigma_{35}^2,$$
$$\bar{D} = \sigma_{41}^2 + \sigma_{42}^2 + \sigma_{43}^2 + \sigma_{44}^2 + \sigma_{45}^2,$$
$$\bar{E} = \sigma_{51}^2 + \sigma_{52}^2 + \sigma_{53}^2 + \sigma_{54}^2 + \sigma_{55}^2,$$
$$\bar{F} = \sigma_{11}\sigma_{21} + \sigma_{12}\sigma_{22} + \sigma_{13}\sigma_{23} + \sigma_{14}\sigma_{24} + \sigma_{15}\sigma_{25},$$
$$\bar{G} = \sigma_{11}\sigma_{31} + \sigma_{12}\sigma_{32} + \sigma_{13}\sigma_{33} + \sigma_{14}\sigma_{34} + \sigma_{15}\sigma_{35},$$
$$\bar{H} = \sigma_{11}\sigma_{41} + \sigma_{12}\sigma_{42} + \sigma_{13}\sigma_{43} + \sigma_{14}\sigma_{44} + \sigma_{15}\sigma_{45},$$
$$\bar{I} = \sigma_{11}\sigma_{51} + \sigma_{12}\sigma_{52} + \sigma_{13}\sigma_{53} + \sigma_{14}\sigma_{54} + \sigma_{15}\sigma_{55},$$
$$\bar{J} = \sigma_{21}\sigma_{31} + \sigma_{22}\sigma_{32} + \sigma_{23}\sigma_{33} + \sigma_{24}\sigma_{34} + \sigma_{25}\sigma_{35},$$
$$\bar{K} = \sigma_{21}\sigma_{41} + \sigma_{22}\sigma_{42} + \sigma_{23}\sigma_{43} + \sigma_{24}\sigma_{44} + \sigma_{25}\sigma_{45},$$
$$\bar{L} = \sigma_{21}\sigma_{51} + \sigma_{22}\sigma_{52} + \sigma_{23}\sigma_{53} + \sigma_{24}\sigma_{54} + \sigma_{25}\sigma_{55},$$
$$\bar{M} = \sigma_{31}\sigma_{41} + \sigma_{32}\sigma_{42} + \sigma_{33}\sigma_{43} + \sigma_{34}\sigma_{44} + \sigma_{35}\sigma_{45},$$
$$\bar{N} = \sigma_{31}\sigma_{51} + \sigma_{32}\sigma_{52} + \sigma_{33}\sigma_{53} + \sigma_{34}\sigma_{54} + \sigma_{35}\sigma_{55},$$
$$\bar{O} = \sigma_{41}\sigma_{51} + \sigma_{42}\sigma_{52} + \sigma_{43}\sigma_{53} + \sigma_{44}\sigma_{54} + \sigma_{45}\sigma_{55}.$$

Empirically, we can identify only the 15 terms $\bar{A}$, $\bar{B}$, $\bar{C}$, $\bar{D}$, $\bar{E}$, $\bar{F}$, $\bar{G}$, $\bar{H}$, $\bar{I}$, $\bar{J}$, $\bar{K}$, $\bar{L}$, $\bar{M}$, $\bar{N}$, and $\bar{O}$. Thus, not all 25 volatility parameters can be identified. This implies that the maximally flexible specification that is well identified has a volatility matrix given by a triangular volatility matrix[1]

$$\Sigma = \begin{pmatrix} \sigma_{11} & 0 & 0 & 0 & 0 \\ \sigma_{21} & \sigma_{22} & 0 & 0 & 0 \\ \sigma_{31} & \sigma_{32} & \sigma_{33} & 0 & 0 \\ \sigma_{41} & \sigma_{42} & \sigma_{43} & \sigma_{44} & 0 \\ \sigma_{51} & \sigma_{52} & \sigma_{53} & \sigma_{54} & \sigma_{55} \end{pmatrix}.$$

---

[1] Note that it can be either upper or lower triangular. The choice is irrelevant for the fit of the model.

Bibliography

Ahn, D.H., R.F. Dittmar, and A.R. Gallant (2002), "Quadratic Term Structure Models: Theory and Evidence," *Review of Financial Studies*, 15, 243–288.

Alfaro, R. (2011), "Affine Nelson-Siegel Model," *Economics Letters*, 110, 1–3.

Almeida, C. (2005), "Affine Processes, Arbitrage-Free Term Structures of Legendre Polynomials, and Option Pricing," *International Journal of Theoretical and Applied Finance*, 8, 161–184.

Almeida, C., A. Duarte, and C. Fernandes (2003), "A Generalization of Principal Components Analysis for Non-Observable Term Structures in Emerging Markets," *International Journal of Theoretical and Applied Finance*, 6, 895–893.

Almeida, C., R. Gomes, A. Leite, A. Simonsen, and J. Vicente (2009), "Does Curvature Enhance Forecasting?" *International Journal of Theoretical and Applied Finance*, 12, 1171–1196.

Almeida, C., A. Simonsen, and J. Vicente (2011), "Forecasting Bond Yields with Segmented Term Structure Models," Manuscript, Getulio Vargas Foundation Graduate School of Economics.

Almeida, C., and J. Vicente (2008), "The Role of No-Arbitrage on Forecasting: Lessons from a Parametric Term Structure Model," *Journal of Banking and Finance*, 32, 2695–2705.

Alper, C.E., K. Kazimov, and A. Akdemir (2007), "Forecasting the Term Structure of Interest Rates for Turkey: A Factor Analysis Approach," *Applied Financial Economics*, 17, 77–85.

Andersen, T.G., and L. Benzoni (2010), "Do Bonds Span Volatility Risk in the US Treasury Market? A Specification Test for Affine Term Structure Models," *Journal of Finance*, 65, 603–653.

Andersen, T.G., T. Bollerslev, P.F. Christoffersen, and F.X. Diebold (2006), "Practical Volatility and Correlation Modeling for Financial Market Risk Management." In M. Carey and R. Stulz (eds.), *The Risks of Financial Institutions*, University of Chicago Press for NBER, 513–548.

Andersen, T.G., T. Bollerslev, and F.X. Diebold (2010), "Parametric and Nonparametric Volatility Measurement." In L.P. Hansen and Y. Aït-Sahalia (eds.), *Handbook of Financial Econometrics*, Elsevier, 67–138.

Andersen, T.G., and J. Lund (1997), "Stochastic Volatility and Mean Drift in the Short Rate Diffusion: Sources of Steepness, Level and Curvature in the Yield Curve," Manuscript, Kellogg School, Northwestern University.

Ang, A., G. Bekaert, and M. Wei (2007), "Do Macro Variables, Asset Markets or Surveys Forecast Inflation Better?" *Journal of Monetary Economics*, 54, 1163–1212.

Ang, A., and M. Piazzesi (2003), "A No-Arbitrage Vector Autoregression of Term Structure Dynamics with Macroeconomic and Latent Variables," *Journal of Monetary Economics*, 50, 745–787.

Aruoba, S.B., and F.X. Diebold (2010), "Real-Time Macroeconomic Monitoring: Real Activity, Inflation, and Interactions," *American Economic Review*, 100, 20–24.

Aruoba, S.B., F.X. Diebold, M.A. Kose, and M.E. Terrones (2011), "Globalization, the Business Cycle, and Macroeconomic Monitoring." In R. Clarida and F.Giavazzi (eds.), *NBER International Seminar on Macroeconomics*, University of Chicago Press.

Aruoba, S.B., F.X. Diebold, and C. Scotti (2009), "Real Time Measurement of Business Conditions," *Journal of Business and Economic Statistics*, 27, 417–427.

Backus, D., A. Gregory, and S. Zin (1989), "Risk Premiums in the Term Structure," *Journal of Monetary Economics*, 24, 371–399.

Balduzzi, P., S.R. Das, S. Foresi, and R.K. Sundaram (1996), "A Simple Approach to Three-Factor Affine Term Structure Models," *Journal of Fixed Income*, 6, 43–53.

Bansal, R., and I. Shaliastovich (2010), "A Long-Run Risks Explanation of Predictability Puzzles in Bond and Currency Markets," Manuscript, Duke University.

Bates, D. (1999), "Financial Markets' Assessment of EMU," *Carnegie-Rochester Conference Series on Public Policy*, 51, 229–269.

Bauer, M.D., and G.D. Rudebusch (2011), "The Signaling Channel for Federal Reserve Bond Purchases," Federal Reserve Bank of San Francisco, Working Paper 2011-21.

Bekaert, G., S. Cho, and A. Moreno (2010), "New-Keynesian Macroeconomics and the Term Structure," *Journal of Money, Credit and Banking*, 42, 33–62.

Bernadell, C., J. Coche, and K. Nyholm (2005), "Yield Curve Prediction for the Strategic Investor," European Central Bank Working Paper No. 472.

Bernanke, B., and J. Boivin (2003), "Monetary Policy in a Data-Rich Environment," *Journal of Monetary Economics*, 50, 525–546.

Bernanke, B.S., J. Boivin, and P. Eliasz (2005), "Measuring the Effects of Monetary Policy: A Factor-Augmented Vector Autoregressive (FAVAR) Approach," *Quarterly Journal of Economics*, 120, 387–422.

Bianchi, F., H. Mumtaz, and P. Surico (2009), "The Great Moderation of the Term Structure of U.K. Interest Rates," *Journal of Monetary Economics*, 56, 856–871.

Bibkov, R., and M. Chernov (2010), "No-Arbitrage Macroeconomic Determinants of the Yield Curve," *Journal of Econometrics*, 159, 166–182.

BIS (2005), "Zero-Coupon Yield Curves: Technical Documentation," BIS Papers No. 25, Bank for International Settlements.

Björk, T., and B.J. Christensen (1999), "Interest Rate Dynamics and Consistent Forward Rate Curves," *Mathematical Finance*, 9, 323–348.

Bliss, R. (1997), "Movements in the Term Structure of Interest Rates," *Federal Reserve Bank of Atlanta Economic Review*, 16–33.

Bohm-Bawerk, E. (1889), *Capital and Interest*, Macmillan.

Bowsher, C.G., and R. Meeks (2008), "The Dynamics of Economic Functions: Modeling and Forecasting the Yield Curve," *Journal of the American Statistical Association*, 103, 1419–1437.

Brüggemann, R., W. Härdle, J. Mungo, and C. Trenkler (2008), "VAR Modeling for Dynamic Semiparametric Factors of Volatility Strings," *Journal of Financial Econometrics*, 6, 361–381.

Calvet, L.E., A.J. Fischer, and L. Wu (2010), "Dimension-Invariant Dynamic Term Structures," Manuscript, HEC Paris, UBS, and Baruch College.

Campbell, J., and J. Cochrane (1999), "By Force of Habit: A Consumption-Based Explanation of Aggregate Stock Market Behavior," *Journal of Political Economy*, 107, 205–251.

Campbell, J., A. Lo, and A. MacKinlay (1997), *The Economics of Financial Markets*, Princeton University Press.

Campbell, J.Y., and R.J. Shiller (1991), "Yield Spreads and Interest Rate Movements: A Bird's Eye View," *Review of Economic Studies*, 495–514.

Campbell, J.Y., and G.B. Tacksler (2003), "Equity Volatility and Corporate Bond Yields," *Journal of Finance*, 58, 2321–2350.

Carriero, A. (2011), "Forecasting the Yield Curve Using Priors from No-Arbitrage Affine Term Structure Models," *International Economic Review*, 52, 425–459.

Carriero, A., C.A. Favero, and I. Kaminska (2006), "Financial Factors, Macroeconomic Information and the Expectations Theory of the Term Structure of Interest Rates," *Journal of Econometrics*, 131, 339–358.

Carriero, A., and R. Giacomini (2011), "How Useful are No-Arbitrage Restrictions for Forecasting the Yield Curve?" *Journal of Econometrics*, in press.

Carriero, A., G. Kapetanios, and M. Marcellino (2010), "Forecasting Government Bond Yields with Large Bayesian VARs," School of Economics and Finance Working Paper 662, Queen Mary College, University of London.

Carter, C.K., and R. Kohn (1994), "On Gibbs Sampling for State Space Models," *Biometrika*, 81, 541–553.

Cassola, N., and N. Porter (2011), "Understanding Chinese Bond Yields and Their Role in Monetary Policy," IMF Working Paper 11/225.

Chambers, D., W. Carleton, and R. McEnally (1988), "Immunizing Default-Free Bond Portfolios with a Duration Vector," *Journal of Financial and Quantitative Analysis*, 23, 89–104.

Chauvet, M., and Z. Senyuz (2009), "A Joint Dynamic Bi-Factor Model of the Yield Curve and the Economy as a Predictor of Business Cycles," Manuscript, University of California–Riverside and University of New Hampshire.

Chen, L. (1996), *Stochastic Mean and Stochastic Volatility*, Blackwell.

Chen, Y., and K. Tsang (2009), "What Does the Yield Curve Tell Us about Exchange Rate Predictability?" Manuscript, University of Washington and Virginia Tech.

Chen, Y., and K. Tsang (2010), "Risk vs. Expectations in Exchange Rate Determination: A Macro-Finance Approach," Manuscript, University of Washington and Virginia Tech.

Chernozhukov, V., and H. Hong (2003), "An MCMC Approach to Classical Estimation," *Journal of Econometrics*, 115, 293–346.

Christensen, J.H.E., F.X. Diebold, and G.D. Rudebusch (2009), "An Arbitrage-Free Generalized Nelson-Siegel Term Structure Model," *Econometrics Journal*, 12, 33–64.

Christensen, J.H.E., F.X. Diebold, and G.D. Rudebusch (2011a), "The Affine Arbitrage-Free Class of Nelson-Siegel Term Structure Models," *Journal of Econometrics*, 164, 4–20.

Christensen, J.H.E., and J.A. Lopez (2011), "Common Risk Factors in the U.S. Treasury and Corporate Bond Markets: An Arbitrage-Free Dynamic Nelson-Siegel Modeling Approach," Manuscript, Federal Reserve Bank of San Francisco.

Christensen, J.H.E., J.A. Lopez, and G.D. Rudebusch (2010a), "Can Term Structure Factors Span Stochastic Volatility?" Manuscript, Federal Reserve Bank of San Francisco.

Christensen, J.H.E., J.A. Lopez, and G.D. Rudebusch (2010b), "Do Central Bank Liquidity Facilities Affect Interbank Lending Rates?" Manuscript, Federal Reserve Bank of San Francisco.

Christensen, J.H.E., J.A. Lopez, and G.D. Rudebusch (2010c), "Inflation Expectations and Risk Premiums in an Arbitrage-Free Model of Nominal and Real Bond Yields," *Journal of Money, Credit, and Banking*, 42, 143–178.

Christensen, J.H.E., J.A. Lopez, and G.D. Rudebusch (2011b), "Extracting Deflation Probability Forecasts from Treasury Yields," Manuscript, Federal Reserve Bank of San Francisco, forthcoming in *International Journal of Central Banking*.

Christensen, J.H.E., and G.D. Rudebusch (2012), "The Response of Government Yields to Central Bank Purchases of Long-Term Bonds," Manuscript, Federal Reserve Bank of San Francisco, forthcoming in *Economic Journal*.

Chua, C.T., D. Foster, K. Ramaswamy, and R. Stine (2008), "A Dynamic Model for the Forward Curve," *Review of Financial Studies*, 21, 265–310.

Cieslak, A., and P. Pavola (2011), "Understanding Bond Risk Premia," Manuscript, University of Lugano and Northwestern University.

Cochrane, J. (2001), *Asset Pricing*, Princeton University Press.

Cochrane, J.H., and M. Piazzesi (2005), "Bond Risk Premia," *American Economic Review*, 95, 138–160.

Collin-Dufresne, P., R.S. Goldstein, and C.S. Jones (2008), "Identification of Maximal Affine Term Structure Models," *Journal of Finance*, 63, 743–795.

Coroneo, L., K. Nyholm, and R. Vidova-Koleva (2011), "How Arbitrage-Free Is the Nelson-Siegel Model?" *Journal of Empirical Finance*, 18, 393–407.

Cox, J.C., J.E. Ingersoll, and S.A. Ross (1985), "A Theory of the Term Structure of Interest Rates," *Econometrica*, 53, 385–407.

Dai, Q., and K.J. Singleton (2000), "Specification Analysis of Affine Term Structure Models," *Journal of Finance*, 55, 1943–1978.

Dai, Q., and K.J. Singleton (2002), "Expectation Puzzles, Time-Varying Risk Premia, and Affine Models of the Term Structure," *Journal of Financial Economics*, 63, 415–441.

D'Amico, S., and T.B. King (2010), "Flow and Stock Effects of Large-Scale Treasury Purchases," Finance and Economics Discussion Series Paper No. 2010-52, Federal Reserve Board.

De Pooter, M. (2007), "Examining the Nelson-Siegel Class of Term Structure Models: In-Sample Fit versus Out-of-Sample Forecasting Performance," Discussion Paper 2007-043/4, Tinbergen Institute, Erasmus University.

De Pooter, M., F. Ravazzolo, and D. van Dijk (2010), "Term Structure Forecasting Using Macro Factors and Forecast Combination," International Finance Discussion Paper No. 2010-993, Federal Reserve Board.

Dempster, A.P., N.M. Laird, and D.B. Rubin (1977), "Maximum Likelihood from Incomplete Data via the EM Algorithm," *Journal of the Royal Statistical Society, Series B*, 39, 1–38.

Dewachter, H., and M. Lyrio (2006), "Macro Factors and the Term Structure of Interest Rates," *Journal of Money Credit and Banking*, 38, 119–140.

Dewachter, H., and M. Lyrio (2008), "Learning, Macroeconomic Dynamics and the Term Structure of Interest Rates." In J. Campbell (ed.), *Asset Prices and Monetary Policy*, University of Chicago Press.

Diebold, F.X. (2003), "Big Data Dynamic Factor Models for Macroeconomic Measurement and Forecasting." In M. Dewatripont, L.P. Hansen, and S. Turnovsky (eds.), *Advances in Economics and Econometrics: Theory and Applications, Eighth World Congress of the Econometric Society*, Cambridge University Press, 115–122.

Diebold, F.X. (2007), *Elements of Forecasting*, Thomson South-Western Publishing, 4th ed.

Diebold, F.X., and L. Kilian (2001), "Measuring Predictability: Theory and Macroeconomic Applications," *Journal of Applied Econometrics*, 16, 657–669.

Diebold, F.X., J.H. Lee, and G. Weinbach (1994), "Regime Switching with Time-Varying Transition Probabilities." In C. Hargreaves (ed.), *Nonstationary Time Series Analysis and Cointegration*, Oxford University Press, 283–302.

Diebold, F.X., and C. Li (2006), "Forecasting the Term Structure of Government Bond Yields," *Journal of Econometrics*, 130, 337–364.

Diebold, F.X., C. Li, and L. Ji (2006a), "A Three-Factor Yield Curve Model: Non-Affine Structure, Systematic Risk Sources, and Generalized Duration." In L.R. Klein (ed.), *Long-Run Growth and Short-Run Stabilization: Essays in Memory of Albert Ando*, Edward Elgar, 240–274.

Diebold, F.X., C. Li, and V. Yue (2008), "Global Yield Curve Dynamics and Interactions: A Generalized Nelson-Siegel Approach," *Journal of Econometrics*, 146, 351–363.

Diebold, F.X., M. Piazzesi, and G.D. Rudebusch (2005), "Modeling Bond Yields in Finance and Macroeconomics," *American Economic Review*, 95, 415–420.

Diebold, F.X., and G.D. Rudebusch (1989), "Scoring the Leading Indicators," *Journal of Business*, 62, 369–391.

Diebold, F.X., and G.D. Rudebusch (1996), "Measuring Business Cycles: A Modern Perspective," *Review of Economics and Statistics*, 78, 67–77.

Diebold, F.X., G.D. Rudebusch, and S.B. Aruoba (2006b), "The Macroeconomy and the Yield Curve: A Dynamic Latent Factor Approach," *Journal of Econometrics*, 131, 309–338.

Diebold, F.X., and K. Yilmaz (2010), "Macroeconomic Volatility and Stock Market Volatility, Worldwide." In T. Bollerslev, J. Russell, and M. Watson (eds.), *Volatility and Time Series Econometrics: Essays in Honor of Robert F. Engle*, Oxford University Press, 97–116.

Doan, T., R. Litterman, and C.A. Sims (1984), "Forecasting and Conditional Projections Using Realistic Prior Distributions," *Econometric Reviews*, 3, 1–100.

Duffee, G.R. (2002), "Term Premia and Interest Rate Forecasts in Affine Models," *Journal of Finance*, 57, 405–443.

Duffee, G.R. (2010), "Sharpe Ratios in Term Structure Models," Manuscript, Johns Hopkins University.

Duffee, G.R. (2011a), "Forecasting with the Term Structure: The Role of No-Arbitrage," Manuscript, Johns Hopkins University.

Duffee, G.R. (2011b), "Information in (and not in) the Term Structure," *Review of Financial Studies*, in press.

Duffie, D., and R. Kan (1996), "A Yield-Factor Model of Interest Rates," *Mathematical Finance*, 6, 379–406.

Duffie, D., J. Pan, and K. Singleton (2000), "Transform Analysis and Asset Pricing for Affine Jump-Diffusions," *Econometrica*, 68, 1343–1376.

Dungey, M., V.L. Martin, and A.R. Pagan (2000), "A Multivariate Latent Factor Decomposition of International Bond Yield Spreads," *Journal of Applied Econometrics*, 15, 697–715.

Durand, D. (1958), "A Quarterly Series of Corporate Basic Yields, 1952–57, and Some Attendant Reservations," *Journal of Finance*, 13, 348–356.

Eggertsson, G.B., and M. Woodford (2003), "The Zero Bound on Interest Rates and Optimal Monetary Policy," *Brookings Papers on Economic Activity*, 34, 139–235.

Epstein, L., and S.E. Zin (1989), "Substitution, Risk Aversion and the Temporal Behavior of Consumption and Asset Returns: A Theoretical Framework," *Econometrica*, 57, 937–969.

Estrella, A., and F.S. Mishkin (1998), "Predicting U.S. Recessions: Financial Variables as Leading Indicators," *Review of Economics and Statistics*, 80, 45–61.

Fabozzi, F.J., L. Martellini, and P. Priaulet (2005), "Predictability in the Shape of the Term Structure of Interest Rates," *Journal of Fixed Income*, June, 40–53.

Fama, E.F., and R.R. Bliss (1987), "The Information in Long-Maturity Forward Rates," *American Economic Review*, 77, 680–692.

Fama, E.F., and K.R. French (1992), "The Cross-Section of Expected Stock Returns," *Journal of Finance*, 47, 427–465.

Favero, C.A., L. Niu, L. Sala, and V. Salasco (2011), "Term Structure Forecasting: No-Arbitrage Restrictions vs. Large Information Sets," *International Journal of Forecasting*, in press.

Fengler, M.R., W. Härdle, and E. Mammen (2007), "A Dynamic Semiparametric Factor Model for Implied Volatility Surface Dynamics," *Journal of Financial Econometrics*, 5, 189–218.

Fengler, M.R., W. Härdle, and P. Schmidt (2002), "The Analysis of Implied Volatilities." In W. Härdle, T. Kleinow, and G. Stahl (eds.), *Applied Quantitative Finance: Theory and Computational Tools*, Springer, 127–137.

Filipović, D. (1999), "A Note on the Nelson-Siegel Family," *Mathematical Finance*, 9, 349–359.

Filipović, D. (2000), "Exponential-Polynomial Families and the Term Structure of Interest Rates," *Bernoulli*, 6, 1081–1107.

Filipović, D. (2009), *Term Structure Models*, Springer-Verlag.

Fisher, I. (1930), *The Theory of Interest*, Porcupine Press.

Fisher, M., D. Nychka, and D. Zervos (1995), "Fitting the Term Structure of Interest Rates with Smoothing Splines," Finance and Economics Discussion Series Paper No. 95-1, Federal Reserve Board.

Fisher, M. and C. Gilles (1996), "Term Premia in Exponential-Affine Models of the Term Structure," Manuscript, Board of Governors of the Federal Reserve System.

Fontaine, J.S., and R. Garcia (2008), "Bond Liquidity Premia," Manuscript, EDHEC Business School, Nice, France.

Frankel, J.A., and C.S. Lown (1994), "An Indicator of Future Inflation Extracted from the Steepness of the Interest Rate Yield Curve along Its Entire Length," *Quarterly Journal of Economics*, 109, 517–530.

Fulop, A. (2009), "Filtering Methods," Manuscript, ESSEC Business School, Paris.

Gabaix, X. (2007), "Linearity-Generating Processes: A Modelling Tool Yielding Closed Forms for Asset Prices," Manuscript, Stern School, New York University.

Gagnon, J., M. Raskin, J. Remache, and B. Sack (2011), "The Financial Market Effects of the Federal Reserve's Large-Scale Asset Purchases," *International Journal of Central Banking*, 7, 3–43.

Gallmeyer, M.F., B. Hollifield, and S.E. Zin (2005), "Taylor Rules, McCallum Rules and the Term Structure of Interest Rates," *Journal of Monetary Economics*, 52, 921–950.

Garbade, K.D. (1999), *Fixed Income Analytics*, MIT Press.

Geweke, J.F. (1977), "The Dynamic Factor Analysis of Economic Time Series Models." In D. Aigner and A. Goldberger (eds.), *Latent Variables in Socioeconomic Models*, North Holland, 365–383.

Giese, J. (2008), "Level, Slope, Curvature: Characterizing the Yield Curve in a Cointegrated VAR Model," *Economics: The Open-Access, Open-Assessment E-Journal*, 2, 2008–2028.

Gimeno, R., and J.M. Marqués (2009), "Extraction of Financial Market Expectations about Inflation and Interest Rates from a Liquid Market," Banco de España Working Paper 0906.

Giordani, P., M.K. Pitt, and R. Kohn (2011), "Bayesian Inference for Time Series State Space Models." In J. Geweke, G. Koop, and H. van Dijk (eds.), *Handbook of Bayesian Econometrics*, Oxford University Press, in press.

Golinski, A., and P. Zaffaroni (2011), "Long Memory Affine Term Structure Models," Manuscript, Imperial College London.

Gourieroux, C., and R. Sufana (2003), "Wishart Quadratic Term Structure Models," HEC Montreal, CREF Working Paper 03-10.

Granger, C.W.J. (1980), "Long Memory Relationships and the Aggregation of Dynamic Models," *Journal of Econometrics*, 14, 227–238.

Gregory, A.W., A.C. Head, and J. Reynauld (1997), "Measuring World Business Cycles," *International Economic Review*, 38, 677–701.

Guidolin, M., and A. Timmermann (2009), "Forecasts of U.S. Short-Term Interest Rates: A Flexible Forecast Combination Approach," *Journal of Financial Economics*, 14, 71–100.

Gürkaynak, R.S., B. Sack, and J.H. Wright (2007), "The US Treasury Yield Curve: 1961 to the Present," *Journal of Monetary Economics*, 54, 2291–2304.

Hamilton, J.D. (1989), "A New Approach to the Economic Analysis of Nonstationary Time Series and the Business Cycle," *Econometrica*, 57, 357–384.

Hamilton, J.D., and C. Wu (2010a), "The Effectiveness of Alternative Monetary Policy Tools in a Zero Lower Bound Environment," Manuscript, University of California–San Diego.

Hamilton, J.D., and C. Wu (2010b), "Identification and Estimation of Gaussian Affine Term Structure Models," Manuscript, University of California–San Diego.

Hamilton, J.D., and C. Wu (2011), "Testable Implications of Affine Term Structure Models," Manuscript, UCSD.

Harvey, A. (1990), *The Econometric Analysis of Time Series*, MIT Press.

Harvey, A., E. Ruiz, and E. Sentana (1992), "Unobserved Component Time Series Models with ARCH Disturbances," *Journal of Econometrics*, 52, 129–157.

Hautsch, N., and Y. Ou (2008), "Yield Curve Factors, Term Structure Volatility, and Bond Risk Premia," SFB 649 Discussion Paper, Humboldt University, Berlin.

Hautsch, N., and F. Yang (2010), "Bayesian Inference in a Stochastic Volatility Nelson-Siegel Model," *Computational Statistics and Data Analysis*, in press. SFB 649 Discussion Paper, Humboldt University, Berlin.

Heath, D., R. Jarrow, and A. Morton (1992), "Bond Pricing and the Term Structure of Interest Rates: A New Methodology for Contingent Claims Valuation," *Econometrica*, 77–105.

Hicks, J.R. (1946), *Value and Capital*, Clarendon, 2nd ed.

Hoffmaister, A.W., J. Roldos, and A. Tuladhar (2010), "Yield Curve Dynamics and Spillovers in Central and Eastern European Countries," IMF Working Paper No. 10/51.

Hördahl, P., O. Tristani, and D. Vestin (2006), "A Joint Econometric Model of Macroeconomic and Term-Structure Dynamics," *Journal of Econometrics*, 131, 405–444.

Hördahl, P., O. Tristani, and D. Vestin (2008), "The Yield Curve and Macroeconomic Dynamics," *Economic Journal*, 118, 1937–1970.

Hua, J. (2010a), "Essays in Financial Econometrics," Ph.D. Dissertation, University of Pennsylvania.

Hua, J. (2010b), "Option Implied Volatilities and Corporate Bond Yields: A Dynamic Factor Approach," Manuscript, Baruch College, City University of New York.

Ingram, B., and C. Whiteman (1994), "Supplanting the Minnesota Prior: Forecasting Macroeconomic Time Series Using Real Business Cycle Priors," *Journal of Monetary Economics*, 34, 497–510.

Jacobs, K., and L. Karoui (2009), "Conditional Volatility in Affine Term Structure Models: Evidence from Treasury and Swap Markets," *Journal of Financial Economics*, 77, 288–318.

Jardet, C., A. Monfort, and F. Pegoraro (2010), "No-Arbitrage Near-Integrated Term Structure Models, Term Premia, and GDP Growth," Manuscript, Bank of France.

Joslin, S., A. Le, and K.J. Singleton (2011a), "Why Gaussian Macro-Finance Term Structure Models Are (Nearly) Unconstrained Factor-VARs," Manuscript, University of Southern California, University of North Carolina, and Stanford University.

Joslin, S., M. Priebsch, and K.J. Singleton (2009), "Risk Premium Accounting in Macro-Dynamic Term Structure Models," Manuscript, MIT and Stanford University.

Joslin, S., M. Priebsch, and K.J. Singleton (2010), "Risk Premiums in Dynamic Term Structure Models with Unspanned Macro Risks," Manuscript, MIT and Stanford University.

Joslin, S., K.J. Singleton, and H. Zhu (2011b), "A New Perspective on Gaussian Dynamic Term Structure Models," *Review of Financial Studies*, 24, 926–970.

Jungbacker, B., and S.J. Koopman (2008), "Likelihood-Based Analysis for Dynamic Factor Models," Tinbergen Institute Discussion Paper TI 2008-0007/4.

Jungbacker, B., S.J. Koopman, and M. van der Wel (2010), "Smooth Dynamic Factor Analysis with an Application to the U.S. Term Structure of Interest Rates," Manuscript, Free University of Amsterdam, Tinbergen Institute, and Erasmus University Rotterdam.

Kessel, R.A. (1965), *The Cyclical Behavior of the Term Structure of Interest Rates*, National Bureau of Economic Research.

Keynes, J.M. (1936), *The General Theory of Employment, Interest, and Money*, Harcourt, Brace and World.

Kim, C.-J., and C.R. Nelson (1999), "Has the U.S. Economy Become More Stable? A Bayesian Approach Based on a Markov-Switching Model of the Business Cycle," *Review of Economics and Statistics*, 81, 608–616.

Kim, D.H., and K.J. Singleton (2012), "Term Structure Models and the Zero Bound: An Empirical Investigation of Japanese Yields," *Journal of Econometrics*, 170, 32–49.

Koivu, M., K. Nyholm, and J. Stromberg (2007a), "Joint Modelling of International Yield Curves," Manuscript, European Central Bank.

Koivu, M., K. Nyholm, and J. Stromberg (2007b), "The Yield Curve and Macro Fundamentals in Forecasting Exchange Rates," *Journal of Financial Forecasting*, 1, 63–83.

Koop, G. (2003), *Bayesian Econometrics*, Wiley.

Koopman, S.J., and J. Durbin (2000), "Fast Filtering and Smoothing for Multivariate State Space Models," *Journal of Time Series Analysis*, 21, 281–296.

Koopman, S.J., M.I.P. Mallee, and M. Van der Wel (2010a), "Analyzing the Term Structure of Interest Rates Using the Dynamic Nelson-Siegel Model with Time-Varying Parameters," *Journal of Business and Economic Statistics*, 28, 329–343.

Koopman, S.J., and N. Shephard (1992), "Exact Score for Time Series Models in State Space Form," *Biometrika*, 79, 823–826.

Koopman, S.J., D. van Dijk, M. Van der Wel, and J.H. Wright (2010b), "Forecasting Interest Rates with Shifting Endpoints," Manuscript, Free University of Amsterdam, Erasmus University Rotterdam, and Johns Hopkins University.

Kose, M.A., C. Otrok, and C.H. Whiteman (2008), "Understanding the Evolution of World Business Cycles," *Journal of International Economics*, 75, 110–130.

Kozicki, S., and P.A. Tinsley (2001), "Shifting Endpoints in the Term Structure of Interest Rates," *Journal of Monetary Economics*, 47, 613–652.

Krippner, L. (2006), "A Theoretically Consistent Version of the Nelson-Siegel Class of Yield Curve Models," *Applied Mathematical Finance*, 13, 39–59.

Krippner, L. (2011a), "Modifying Gaussian Term Structure Models when Interest Rates Are Near the Zero Lower Bound," Manuscript, Reserve Bank of New Zealand.

Krippner, L. (2011b), "A Theoretical Foundation for the Nelson-Siegel Class of Yield Curve Models," Revised Manuscript, Reserve Bank of New Zealand (originally issued as Discussion Paper 2009/10).

Krishnan, C.N.V., P. Ritchken, and J. Thomson (2010), "Predicting Credit Spreads," *Journal of Financial Intermediation*, 19, 529–563.

Kurmann, A., and C. Otrok (2010), "News Shocks and the Slope of the Term Structure of Interest Rates," Manuscript, University of Quebec and University of Virginia.

Langetieg, T.C. (1980), "A Multivariate Model of the Term Structure," *Journal of Finance*, 35, 71–97.

Laurini, M.P., and L.K. Hotta (2010), "Bayesian Extensions of the Diebold and Li Term Structure Model," *International Review of Financial Analysis*, 19, 342–350.

Lengwiler, Y., and C. Lenz (2010), "Intelligible Factors for the Yield Curve," *Journal of Econometrics*, 157, 481–491.

Litterman, R., and J.A. Scheinkman (1991), "Common Factors Affecting Bond Returns," *Journal of Fixed Income*, 1, 77–85.

Litterman, R., J.A. Scheinkman, and L. Weiss (1991), "Volatility and the Yield Curve," *Journal of Fixed Income*, 1, 49–53.

Litzenberger, R., G. Squassi, and N. Weir (1995), "Spline Models of the Term Structure of Interest Rates and Their Applications," Working paper, Goldman Sachs.

Ludvigson, S.C., and S. Ng (2009), "Macro Factors in Bond Risk Premia," *Review of Financial Studies*, 22, 5027–5067.

Macaulay, F. (1938), *Some Theoretical Problems Suggested by the Movements of Interest Rates, Bond Yields, and Stock Prices in the United States Since 1865*, National Bureau of Economic Research.

Malkiel, B.G. (1966), *The Term Structure of Interest Rates*, Princeton University Press.

McCulloch, J.H. (1971), "Measuring the Term Structure of Interest Rates," *Journal of Business*, 44, 19–31.

McCulloch, J.H. (1975), *Money and Inflation: A Monetarist Approach*, Academic Press.

McCulloch, J.H., and H.C. Kwon (1993), "U.S. Term Structure Data, 1947–1991," Working Paper 93-6, Ohio State University.

Meiselman, D. (1962), *The Term Structure of Interest Rates*, Prentice-Hall.

Merton, R.C. (1974), "On the Pricing of Corporate Debt: The Risk Structure of Interest Rates," *Journal of Finance*, 29, 449–470.

Modigliani, F., and R. Sutch (1967), "Debt Management and the Term Structure of Interest Rates: An Empirical Analysis of Recent Experience," *Journal of Political Economy*, 75, 569–589.

Mönch, E. (2008), "Forecasting the Yield Curve in a Data-Rich Environment: A No-Arbitrage Factor-Augmented VAR Approach," *Journal of Econometrics*, 146, 26–43.

Neftci, S.N. (2004), *Financial Engineering*, Academic Press.

Nelson, C.R. (1972), *The Term Structure of Interest Rates*, Basic Books.

Nelson, C.R., and A.F. Siegel (1987), "Parsimonious Modeling of Yield Curves," *Journal of Business*, 473–489.

Nyholm, K. (2007), "A New Approach to Predicting Recessions," *Economic Notes*, 36, 27–42.

Nyholm, K. (2008), *Strategic Asset Allocation in Fixed-Income Markets: A Matlab-Based User's Guide*, Wiley.

Nyholm, K., and R. Rebonato (2008), "Long-Horizon Yield Curve Projections: Comparison of Semi-parametric and Parametric Approaches," *Applied Financial Economics*, 18, 1597–1611.

Nyholm, K., and R. Vidova-Koleva (2011), "Nelson-Siegel, Affine and Quadratic Yield Curve Specifications: Which One Is Better at Forecasting?" *Journal of Forecasting*, in press.

Pagan, A. (1984), "Econometric Issues in the Analysis of Regressions with Generated Regressors," *International Economic Review*, 25, 221–247.

Park, B., E. Mammen, W. Härdle, and S. Borak (2009), "Time Series Modelling with Semiparametric Factor Dynamics," *Journal of the American Statistical Association*, 104, 284–298.

Piazzesi, M. (2010), "Affine Term Structure Models." In L.P. Hansen and Y. Aït-Sahalia (eds.), *Handbook of Financial Econometrics*, Elsevier, 691–766.

Piazzesi, M., and M. Schneider (2006), "Equilibrium Yield Curves," *NBER Macro Annual*, 389–442.

Ramsay, J.O., G. Hooker, and S. Graves (2009), *Functional Data Analysis with R and Matlab*, Springer.

Ramsay, J.O., and B.W. Silverman (2005), *Functional Data Analysis*, Springer, 2nd ed.

Reis, R., and M.W. Watson (2010), "Relative Goods' Prices, Pure Inflation, and the Phillips Correlation," *American Economic Journal: Macroeconomics*, 2, 128–157.

Rudebusch, G., and T. Wu (2008), "A Macro-Finance Model of the Term Structure, Monetary Policy and the Economy," *Economic Journal*, 118, 906–926.

Rudebusch, G.D., and E. Swanson (2012), "The Bond Premium in a DSGE Model with Long-Run Real and Nominal Risks," *American Economic Journal: Macroeconomics*, 4, 105–143.

Rudebusch, G.D., and E.T. Swanson (2008), "Examining the Bond Premium Puzzle with a DSGE Model," *Journal of Monetary Economics*, 55, S111–S126.

Rudebusch, G.D., E.T. Swanson, and T. Wu (2006), "The Bond Yield 'Conundrum' from a Macro-Finance Perspective," *Monetary and Economic Studies*, 24, 83–128.

Rudebusch, G.D., and T. Wu (2007), "Accounting for a Shift in Term Structure Behavior with No-Arbitrage and Macro-Finance Models," *Journal of Money, Credit and Banking*, 39, 395–422.

Sargent, T.J., and C.A. Sims (1977), "Business Cycle Modeling without Pretending to Have Too Much A Priori Theory." In C.A. Sims (ed.), *New Methods in Business Cycle Research: Proceedings from a Conference*, Federal Reserve Bank of Minneapolis, 45–109.

Schorfheide, F. (2011), "Estimation and Evaluation of DSGE Models: Progress and Challenges." In D. Acemoglu, M. Arellano, and E. Dekel (eds.), *Advances in Economics and Econometrics: Theory and Applications, Tenth World Congress of the Econometric Society*, Cambridge University Press, in press.

Sharef, E., and D. Filipović (2004), "Conditions for Consistent Exponential-Polynomial Forward Rate Processes with Multiple Nontrivial Factors," *International Journal of Theoretical and Applied Finance*, 7, 685–700.

Shea, G.S. (1984), "Pitfalls in Smoothing Interest Rate Term Structure Data: Equilibrium Models and Spline Approximations," *Journal of Financial and Quantitative Analysis*, 19, 253–269.

Shiller, R.J. (1973), "A Distributed Lag Estimator Derived from Smoothness Priors," *Econometrica*, 41, 775–788.

Siegel, Andrew F. (2009), "Arbitrage-Free Linear Price Function Models for the Term Structure of Interest Rates," Manuscript, University of Washington.

Singleton, K. (2006), *Empirical Dynamic Asset Pricing*, Princeton University Press.

Söderlind, P., and L. Svensson (1997), "New Techniques to Extract Market Expectations from Financial Instruments," *Journal of Monetary Economics*, 40, 383–429.

Steeley, J.M. (2011), "A Shape-Based Decomposition of the Yield Adjustment Term in the Arbitrage-Free Nelson-Siegel (AFNS) Model of the Yield Curve," Manuscript, Aston University.

Stock, J.H., and M.W. Watson (1999), "Forecasting Inflation," *Journal of Monetary Economics*, 44, 293–335.

Stock, J.H., and M.W. Watson (2003), *Introduction to Econometrics*, Boston: Pearson Education.

Svensson, L.E.O. (1995), "Estimating Forward Interest Rates with the Extended Nelson-Siegel Method," *Sveriges Riksbank Quarterly Review*, 3, 13–26.

Tam, C.S., and I.W. Yu (2008), "Modeling Sovereign Bond Yield Curves of the U.S., Japan and Germany," *International Journal of Finance and Economics*, 13, 82–91.

Tanner, M.A. (1993), *Tools for Statistical Inference*, Springer-Verlag.

Trolle, A.B., and E.S. Schwartz (2009), "A General Stochastic Volatility Model for the Pricing of Interest Rate Derivatives," *Review of Financial Studies*, 22, 2007–2057.

van Binsbergen, J.H., J. Fernández-Villaverde, R.S.J. Koijen, and J.F. Rubio-Ramírez (2010), "The Term Structure of Interest Rates in a DSGE Model with Recursive Preferences," NBER Working Paper No. 11380.

Van Horne, J. (1965), "Interest-Rate Risk and the Term Structure of Interest Rates," *Journal of Political Economy*, 73, 344–351.

Vasicek, O. (1977), "An Equilibrium Characterization of the Term Structure," *Journal of Financial Economics*, 5, 177–188.

Vasicek, O.A., and H.G. Fong (1982), "Term Structure Modeling Using Exponential Splines," *Journal of Finance*, 37, 339–348.

Vayanos, D., and J. Vila (2009), "A Preferred-Habitat Model of the Term Structure of Interest Rates," NBER Working Paper 15487.

Wachter, J. (2006), "A Consumption-Based Model of the Term Structure of Interest Rates," *Journal of Financial Economics*, 79, 365–399.

Wallace, N. (1981), "A Modigliani-Miller Theorem for Open-Market Operations," *American Economic Review*, 71, 267–274.

Watson, M.W., and R.F. Engle (1983), "Alternative Algorithms for the Estimation of Dynamic Factor, MIMIC and Varying Coefficient Regression Models," *Journal of Econometrics*, 23, 385–400.

Wei, M., and J.H. Wright (2010), "Reverse Regressions and Long-Horizon Forecasting," Manuscript, Federal Reserve Board and Johns Hopkins University.

Williams, D. (1997), *Probability with Martingales*, Cambridge University Press.

Willner, R. (1996), "A New Tool for Portfolio Managers: Level, Slope and Curvature Durations," *Journal of Fixed Income*, June, 48–59.

Wright, J. (2011), "Term Premia and Inflation Uncertainty: Empirical Evidence from an International Panel Dataset," *American Economic Review*, 101, 1514–1534.

Yu, W., and E.W. Zivot (2011), "Forecasting the Term Structures of Treasury and Corporate Yields Using Dynamic Nelson-Siegel Models," *International Journal of Forecasting*, 27, 579–591.

Yu, W.C., and D.M. Salyards (2009), "Parsimonious Modeling and Forecasting of Corporate Yield Curve," *Journal of Forecasting*, 28, 73–88.

Zantedeschi, D., P. Damien, and N.G. Polson (2011), "Predictive Macro-Finance with Dynamic Partition Models," *Journal of the American Statistical Association*, 106, 427–439.

Index